the new
Zucchini Cookbook

by Nancy C. Ralston and Marynor Jordan

Revised Edition

A Storey Publishing Book

Storey Communications, Inc.
Schoolhouse Road
Pownal, Vermont 05261

*The mission of Storey Communications is to serve our customers
by publishing practical information that encourages personal independence
in harmony with the environment.*

THIS BOOK IS DEDICATED TO DOROTHY KANDRAC

Front cover designed by Dawson Design and Carol Jessop
Line drawings by Carol Jessop
Text designed and produced by Carol Jessop
Edited by Constance Oxley

Copyright © 1990 by Storey Communications, Inc.

All rights reserved. No part of this book may be reproduced without permission in writing from the publisher, except by a reviewer, who may quote brief passages or reproduce illustrations in a review with appropriate credit; nor may any part of this book be reproduced, stored in a retrieval system, or transmitted in any form or by any means — electronic, photocopying, recording, or other — without permission in writing from the publisher.

Storey Publishing books are available for special premium and promotional uses and for customized editions.
For further information please call the Custom Publishing Department at 1-800-793-9396.

Printed in the United States by Capital City Press
20 19 18 17 16 15 14 13 12 11

Library of Congress Cataloging-in-Publication Data

Ralston, Nancy C.
    The new zucchini cookbook / by Nancy C. Ralston and Marynor Jordan. — Rev. ed.
    p. cm.
    (A Garden Way Publishing Classic)
    Revision of: Garden Way's zucchini cookbook. 1977.
    ISBN 0-88266-590-1 — ISBN 0-88266-589-8 (pbk.)
    1. Cookery (Zucchini)   I. Jordan, Marynor.   II. Title.
    TX803.Z82R34   1990
    641.6'562—dc20
                                                                    89-46018
                                                                    CIP

CONTENTS

PREFACE

Too much squash? The greatest problem gardeners have with this fresh vegetable is its frightening productivity. When heat and moisture are ideal, growth is so rapid that the gardener is picking more squash, on a daily basis, than anyone knows how to use.

These recipes and suggested uses for summer and winter squash should make it much easier to answer the question, "What are we going to do with all of this squash?"

Summer squash is edible at any size; however, there are certain preferences depending upon the type of preparation for which it is intended. There are squash "snobs" who never eat a zucchini or any other summer squash which is more than five inches long. These "babies" are, indeed, delicious and some recipes specify small squash. Medium-sized squash from six to nine inches are adaptable to any kind of preparation, from raw snacks for nibbling to the most sophisticated cream soup or soufflé. The "biggies," which are tougher, seedier, less palatable, and less adaptable than younger specimens, are best utilized in bread or other recipes which call for grated squash.

The naive gardener or consumer often equates large size with a healthy, desirable growth rate and economy in production or purchase. While such reasoning may make sense in some circumstances and with some produce, it does not hold true with squash, especially the summer varieties.

Grow lots of squash (it is almost impossible to do otherwise), but remember to pick frequently so that your crop may be cooked at its peak, and realize, there's no such thing as too much squash.

CHAPTER 1

BECOMING ACQUAINTED

FAMILY HISTORY

Members of the cucurbitacce family have helped to feed the natives of this continent since the recording of history. Recent research, using carbon dating on ancient seeds, reveals that squash was grown in this country at least 7,000 years ago.

Hernando de Soto found squash flourishing in what is now Florida. Jacques Cartier found squash in Canada and called it *gros melon*. Samuel de Champlain reported the cultivation of squash in New England. Squash has been around for a very long time; however, until the home gardener discovered zucchini, not much had been said or done with these amazing plants which flourish from coast to coast. No other vegetable exhibits the same diversity and versatility. The large cucurbitacce family includes not only squash, but pumpkins and gourds as well.

The pumpkin, long a holiday staple in the form of pie, is believed to have been served at the very first Thanksgiving dinner. Whether pie was or was not part of the menu on that auspicious occasion is difficult to document, but we are safe in assuming that squash and pumpkin were present in some form and eagerly devoured. The first and simplest of all pumpkin puddings was very easily made by early settlers. The pumpkin was picked, washed, hollowed out, filled with milk or cream, and baked whole.

Edible gourds generally are mistaken for squash and vice versa. The Turk's Turban, for example, is used frequently with other types of gourds in ornamental arrangements. Few people who purchase turbans are aware that it is edible.

THE SQUASH PATCH

Zucchini, one of the "cousins" in the large cucurbitacce family, is related to many other varieties of summer squash, winter squash, edible gourds, and pumpkins. Zucchini recipes generally are suitable for all other summer squash which may be substituted or used in combination. A rather colorful dish, for example, can result from combining the dark green zucchini with its golden cousin or perhaps a crookneck variety.

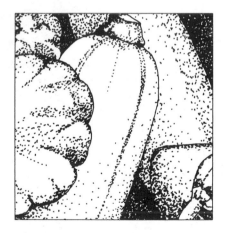

Winter squash also is frequently interchangeable in recipes, and so the squash gardener and cook need not think that all varieties of squash and pumpkin must be available in order to enjoy the full range of squash cooking. In fact, a summer squash, most likely a zucchini, and a tough-skinned winter squash, such as a butternut, plus a pumpkin should provide the cook with all of the basic ingredients to try all the breakfast, lunch, dinner, and snack possibilities included in this book.

SQUASH SCHOOLING

There are two easy ways to learn about squash. One is to consult one or more comprehensive seed catalogues. New editions of these publications become available to the eager gardener by January. Some begin appearing as early as late November. There should be plenty of time to consult the colorful and informative pages of catalogues before the all-important final order is submitted in early spring. The reader will discover more than seventy squash varieties from which to choose and this number does not include thirty some pumpkins and edible gourds. Confusion is compounded every year as botanists continue to develop additional hybrids with new and fascinating names.

The second source of "squash schooling" is supermarkets and roadside produce stands which offer colorful collections of both summer and winter "cousins" during the summer and early fall. Some varieties, because of differing geographical growing conditions, are available almost year-round.

GROWING SQUASH

Two summer squash plants of whatever variety will provide sufficient zucchini, crooknecks, or pattypans to satisfy the members of one household. Four winter squash plants can be relied upon to provide the same satisfaction. Depending upon the size of the family and garden space, judge accordingly when buying seed.

Squash seed remains viable for several years, so do not think that each seed must be planted lest you be wasteful. Save the seed surplus for next year. It pays to prevent overplanting which does lead to a great deal of waste. Either share the contents of a single package with a neighbor, which makes great sense, or place surplus seeds in an airtight container and try not to forget to use them next season.

Saving the seed of mature squash for another season is ill-advised. There may be in a large squash patch, a certain amount of cross fertilization. This type of vegetable "incest" can produce some unusual offspring. These may be edible, but they do not compare favorably with the parent plant. These and volunteer squash plants should be weeded out.

The division of squash into summer and winter categories is confusing because both are planted at the same time. The biggest difference between the two is the length of growing period. Summer squash varieties have growing periods which range from 45-55 days. Winter squash, which must reach maturity before the orange flesh is at its prime, will require garden space from 75-120 days. They are harvested in the fall and may be stored for winter use. Pumpkins and edible gourds fall into this division.

Most winter squash fall into the vining category. In fact, unless a seed packet or catalogue specifically identifies a squash as bush type, the plant will be a space grabber. If adequate garden space is a real problem, the vining squash should be trained to grow on a trellis or tepee. The expansive growth of vining squash can be curtailed by pinching back. Bush types can even be grown in containers, which means it is possible to grow squash on a sunny porch or deck. As for other growing conditions, seed packets always provide planting instructions.

Most squash are space grabbers and may become a nuisance if overplanted. The bush varieties, although prolific, have less of a tendency to play octopus and overtake other planted areas of your garden.

Both summer and winter varieties are susceptible to the ravages of insects, especially the squash borer. When the first blooms appear, the white worms tunnel inside squash stems. Dusting with Rotenone or Sevin will help to discourage these and other pests.

Seed catalogues present choices of both summer and winter squash as well as bush and vining types. Indeed, there must be a squash for everyone, regardless of space requirements.

Many of the recipes in this book can help you deal with the inevitable oversupply, so there is no need for an excessively abundant crop to go to waste.

A later section on preserving and storing squash explains how simple it is to lay away a supply of both summer and winter squash that will last all winter. With a freezer supply of squash combinations, such as those in the chapter VEGETABLE DISHES and other containers of mashed squash, the gardener can pass up the somewhat battered specimens displayed on supermarket counters for unbelievable prices.

SUMMER SQUASH SURPRISES

Zucchini and other summer squash can hide under their foliage where they are capable of expanding to unbelievable dimensions. Generally there is enough of a problem about disposition of surplus squash without finding a supply of monster specimens. It is important to remember that small summer squash are preferable to those which have been allowed to grow until they are beyond their peak in size. Large summer squash are seedy, tough skinned, and not at all at the peak of flavor or texture. Do not be tempted to buy or raise "biggies" with the misguided notion that "big is better." Nothing could be further from the truth.

WINTER SQUASH WISDOM

The slow-growing winter squash, unlike its summer cousins, must be allowed to reach maturity. At that point, thick, tough skin makes it a candidate for winter storage. This squash sweetens with age as the starches turn to sugars. If picked before reaching its prime, the squash pulp will be watery and less than desirable. When the vining winter squash stakes out its claim of garden space, it plans to be there for quite a while.

Vines may extend as much as twenty feet or more. In this sense, the winter squash plant resembles that of the pumpkin more than does its other cousin, the summer squash.

GOURD AND PUMPKIN POSSIBILITIES

In some catalogues and in many recipes, gourds, pumpkins, and winter squash are interchangeable. In fact, a pie made with a variety of winter squash is virtually indistinguishable from one made with a Turk's Turban gourd or with a variety of pumpkin. It pays to remember that some gourds are not just ornamental and neither are pumpkins all cut out to be jack-o'-lanterns.

Normally, there are two purposes to be served by the gardener's pumpkin patch. The sugar or sweet pumpkin is counted on to produce the Thanksgiving pie. Younger gardeners in the family are more interested in the traditional jack-o'-lanterns for Halloween, and the bigger the pumpkin, the better. Many pumpkins will keep everyone happy by serving both purposes.

Whatever the primary purpose, the gardener has many varieties from which to choose. In larger gardens, seeds of several types may be sown for comparison purposes. In cases of very limited space, the novel midget varieties are recommended.

ROLL CALL: SQUASH, GOURDS, AND PUMPKINS

The varieties described are current as of June, 1990.

SUMMER SQUASH

Aristocrat

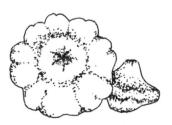

Benning's Green Tint

Apple:
(55 days)

Hybrid of Globe squash. Richer in flavor than most summer squash. Has attractive green-striped fruit. Is a very productive plant.

Arlesa:
(48 days)

Variety of French Courgette. Has thin skin and is very tender. Superior in taste and vigor. Does not become woody with size.

Ambassador:
(50 days)

Hybrid Zucchini. Is at its prime at 8-10 inches. Fruit is waxy and dark green.

Aristocrat:
(50 days)

Hybrid Zucchini. Bushy, vigorous plants produce glossy, dark green fruit. Flesh is crisp, tender, and creamy white. Flavor peaks at 8-10 inches. Grows upright for easier picking.

Benning's Green Tint:
(55 days)

Hybrid, light green Pattypan

Blackmagic:
(50 days)

Hybrid Zucchini. A semibush plant with nearly seedless fruit.

Butterbar:
(49 days)

Hybrid yellow summer squash. Has tender skin.

Butterblossom:
(85 days)

Hybrid Courgette. Is a prolific bearer of large golden blossoms. Use these blossoms in recipes.

Butterstick:
(50 days)

Hybrid yellow squash. Has golden fruit with nutty flavor.

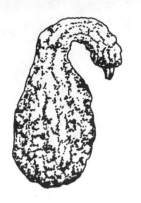

Crookneck

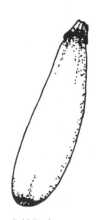

Gold Rush

Butterswan: (50 days)	Hybrid Crookneck squash. Tender fruit.
Cocozelle: (45 days)	Slim, green-striped hybrid Zucchini
Courgette: (48 days)	French Zucchini. Suitable for harvest at 3 inches. May be cooked whole.
Chayote:	See: EDIBLE GOURDS
Crookneck: (53 days)	Warted, bright yellow summer squash
Cymling: (50 days)	A yellow summer squash, such as Straightneck
Daytona: (50 days)	Hybrid Crookneck
Dixie: (45 days)	A very early yellow squash
Eldorado: (49 days)	Hybrid golden Zucchini
Globe: (45-47 days)	Small round fruit perfect for stuffed individual servings. Versatile squash raw, sautéed, or steamed.
Gold Bar: (55 days)	Bushlike plant produces Straightneck yellow fruit. See: Cymling
Golden Girl: (50 days)	Hybrid golden Zucchini
Gold Rush: (45 days)	Hybrid Zucchini with golden skin

Globe

Greyzini

Kuta

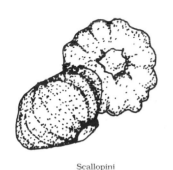

Scallopini

Green Whopper:
(48 days)

Hybrid Zucchini which produces over a long period

Greyzini:
(55 days)

Hybrid Zucchini with longer and more slender fruit

Kuta:
(48 days)

Hybrid, pale green, cylindrical squash. May be harvested as summer squash, or allowed to mature as winter squash when it becomes dark green and thick skinned.

Marrow Twickers:
(68 days)

Oval, green-striped, sturdy hybrid of European favorite marrow squash.

Multipik:
(50 days)

Creamy yellow squash. Early and prolific.

Opo:
(55-60 days)

Oriental squash. Cylindrical shape and light green color, resembles Kuta.

Pattypan:
(55 days)

Bush plant produces white scalloped fruit. Good for stuffing.

Peterpan:
(49 days)

Hybrid Scalloped squash. Light green skin.

Pic-n-pic:
(50 days)

Hybrid Crookneck with wartless skin

Rondo De Nice:
(47 days)

See: Globe squash

Sardane:
(48 days)

Small Italian summer squash. Green fruit often picked small with blossoms attached.

Scallopini:
(50 days)

Hybrid Pattypan. Bush produces light green squash.

Seneca:
(42 days)

Hybrid Zucchini. Does well in cool weather.

Straightneck:
(50 days)

Yellow summer squash. Also called Cymling.

Sunburst:
(55 days)

Scallopini hybrid. Bright yellow skin. Ornamental as well as edible. Buttery fruit remains firm but tender.

Sundance:
(50 days)

Hybrid Crookneck. Has nutty flavor.

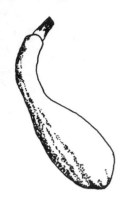

Sundance

Sun Drops:
(48 days)

Space-saving bush produces small, light yellow oval-shaped fruit.

Supersett:
(50 days)

Hybrid Crookneck. Has yellow stem.

Vegetable Marrow:
(55 days)

Favorite of English gardeners. Cylindrical pale green fruit.

White Bush:
(55 days)

French Zucchini. May be prepared as summer squash when small, or winter squash when mature.

Zucchetta Rampicant:
(60 days)

Italian squash. S-shaped, pale green fruit. Has artichoke flavor. Fruit does not become limp when cooked.

Acorn

Zucchini:
(50 days)

Most popular squash in the United States. Has Italian name and French origin. Long, green cylindrical fruit at its best at 4-6 inches.

WINTER SQUASH

Acorn:
(75 days)

Most popular winter squash. Hard-shelled, dark green fruit filled with delicious orange flesh. Halves make perfect individual servings.

Blue Hubbard

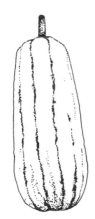

Butternut

Delicata

Banana:
(100 days)

Large cylindrical squash with smooth, pale pink skin. Flesh is very firm and dry. May grow to weigh 25-30 pounds.

Banana Blue:
(105 days)

Large, grey-green fruit. Flesh is deep orange, free from stringy fiber. More resistant to squash bugs than other varieties.

Big Moon:

See: PUMPKINS

Blue Hubbard:
(120 days)

Large, blue, ridged squash. Averages 15 pounds. See also: Hubbard

Butterball:
(95 days)

Grey-green fruit on short vines. Flavor similar to sweet potato. Stores well. A hybrid Sakata.

Butterbush:
(100 days)

Hybrid Butternut

Butter Cup:
(93 days)

Small, dark green turban-shaped fruit. Sweet orange flesh.

Butternut:
(105 days)

Thick-necked squash averaging 4-5 pounds. Small seed cavity at base. Skin is tan and flesh is orange.

Chinese Okra:
(90 days)

See: EDIBLE GOURDS

Cream of the Crop:
(95 days)

Hybrid acorn squash with ivory white skin.

Cushaw:

See: PUMPKINS

Delicata:
(100 days)

Also called Sweet Potato squash. Green-striped fruit excellent for baking and stuffing.

Golden Delicious

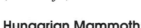

Gold Nugget

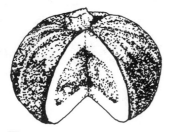

Honey Delight

Ebony Acorn:
(90 days)

Dark skinned hybrid Acorn

Golden Acorn:
(90 days)

Bright yellow hybrid

Golden Delicious:
(102 days)

Golden hybrid with very sweet flesh which is never watery. Good for canning.

Gold Nugget:
(85 days)

Bushy plant produces orange fruits which store well. Fastest growing winter squash.

Honey Delight:
(100 days)

Flattened round fruit of Oriental heritage. Skin is dark green with lighter stripes. Very sweet flesh is orange.

Hubbard:
(100 days)

Average weight 15-25 pounds. Has hard, bumpy, and bluish skin. Excellent for storage.

Hungarian Mammoth:
(110 days)

Weight from 100-200 pounds. Jumbo grey-green squash with orange flesh which is good for freezing.

Kabocha:
(95 days)

Japanese squash. Pale grey-green shell, golden flesh. Ball shape.

Kikuza:
(100 days)

Tan, ribbed fruit 4-4½ pounds. Chinese winter squash of excellent flavor.

Mango Squash:

See: EDIBLE GOURDS

Mirliton:

See: EDIBLE GOURDS

Orangetti:
(85 days)

Orange colored version of Vegetable Spaghetti. Has shorter growing time.

Ponca:
(83 days)

Small, early Butternut hybrid

Red Kuri

Spaghetti Squash

Tahitian Melon

Red Kuri:
(92 days)

Vining Japanese squash. Bright red, weighing 4-7 pounds produced on 7-foot vines.

Sakata:

See: Butterball

Show King:

See: PUMPKINS

Spaghetti Squash:

See: Vegetable Spaghetti

Swan White:
(90 days)

Hybrid white Acorn

Sweet Dumpling:
(100 days)

See: Vegetable Gourd. Similar in color to Delicata but small enough to be single serving size.

Sweet Mama:
(85 days)

Hybrid Butter Cup. Dark green drum-shaped fruit.

Sweet Potato:

See: Delicata

Table Ace:
(78 days)

Hybrid Acorn

Table Queen:
(80 days)

See: Acorn

Table King:
(76 days)

See: Acorn

Tahitian Melon:
(180-200 days)

Sweetest of winter squashes. Large club-shaped fruit may weigh as much as 40 pounds. Raw orange flesh is melon-like. When baked, has yam-like flavor. Does well wherever winter squash is harvested.

Turban:

See: EDIBLE GOURDS

Vegetable Spaghetti:
(100 days)

Unique squash with spaghetti-like flesh. When mature, skin changes from white to yellow. Harvested fruit will keep for two months when properly stored.

EDIBLE GOURDS

Chayote:
(135 days)

Pear-shaped, light green gourd. Cultivated and consumed by Aztecs and Mayans. Needs long hot summer. Frequently identified as squash. To prepare: Remove skin which toughens in cooking and treat as summer squash. Also called Mirlitons or Mango squash.

Sweet Dumpling

Chinese Okra:
(90 days)

Also called Ridged Luffa and Edible Gourd. Harvest at 4-6 inches, remove ridges, and prepare like summer squash.

Cucuzzi:
(70 days)

Italian edible gourd. Often classified as squash. May grow to length of 3 feet at maturity. Also called New Guinea Buttervine. Most palatable at 12 inches when it is prepared in same manner as summer squash.

Lagenaria Longissima:
(65 days)

Used as summer squash when picked half ripe. Has rich full flavor. Does best if supported and allowed to climb.

Mango Squash:

See: Chayote

Mirliton:

See: Chayote

Turk's Turban

New Guinea Buttervine:

See: Cucuzzi

Ridged Luffa:

See: Chinese Okra. Also called Edible Gourd.

Sweet Dumpling:
(100 days)

Also called Vegetable Gourd. Often classified as winter squash. Small striped fruit.

Turk's Turban:
(105 days)

Generally considered to be an ornamental gourd. May be prepared in same manner as winter squash. Bright red and green gourd may grow to be 8-10 inches across.

Vegetable Gourd:

See: Sweet Dumpling

PUMPKINS

Atlantic Giant:
(120 days)

World weight record holder. Not for the small garden. Can grow to weight of 400 or more pounds.

Autumn Gold:
(90 days)

All-America winner. Hybrid which becomes orange in color long before other pumpkins. Averages 9 inches in diameter, three fruits per plant.

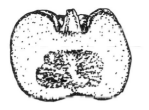

Vegetable Gourd

Baby Pam:
(100 days)

Good for small jack-o'-lanterns. Also for pie making. Fruits are 5 ½ inches in diameter. Flesh is smooth and creamy. Plant produces up to twelve pumpkins.

Big Max:
(120 days)

Giant fruit weighing as much as 100 pounds. Has pinkish skin, yellow flesh. Great for jack-o'-lanterns and lots of pie.

Big Moon:
(120 days)

Too big for average garden. Wins blue ribbons for size. Is really a squash, but looks like and is often sold as a pumpkin.

Calabasa:
(80-90 days)

West Indian variety beginning to appear in American marketplaces. Also popular in the Caribbean, South American, and in some areas of the Mediterranean, where it is called Potiron or Courges.

Autumn Gold

Connecticut Field:
(100 days)

Favorite pumpkin for Halloween. Round and flat on both ends. Average weight is 20 pounds. Flavorful flesh.

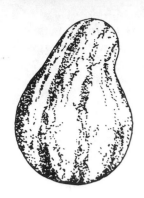

Cushaw

Funny Face

Jack-Be-Little

Courges:	See: Calabasa
Cushaw: (115 days)	Green-striped pumpkin. Looks like a squash and is often sold as such. Cooks like a winter squash. Neck is edible portion. Big round end is seed cavity. Fruit averages 10 pounds.
Funny Face: (90 days)	Semibush hybrid. Good for small gardens. Short season ideal for northern areas. Weighs in from 10-15 pounds. Suitable for baking.
Ghost Rider: (115 days)	Attractive jack-o'-lantern. Strong stem makes good handle. Suitable for canning and freezing.
Howden: (115 days)	Connecticut Field type. Larger and more uniform. A model large pumpkin. Good keeper.
Jack-Be-Little: (100 days)	Tiny edible pumpkin. Great for table decoration. Averages 2 inches in height, 3 inches in diameter.
Little Lantern: (100 days)	Small edible and ornamental fruit
Munchkin Midget:	See: Jack-Be-Little
Pankow's Field: (120 days)	Has thick sturdy stem, suitable for Halloween.
Papaja Pumpkin: (90 days)	Dark green with yellow mottling. This Asian pumpkin resembles the papaya.
Potiron:	See: Calabasa
Show King: (115 days)	Blue-ribbon winner at 466 pounds. Actually a squash, the fruit looks like a large white pumpkin.

Sweetie Pie:
(110 days)

Midget pumpkin. Is a delicacy in China where seed originated.

Tallman:
(110 days)

Bruise tolerant pumpkin. Color deep orange. Upright shape is good for Halloween.

SPEAKING NUTRITIONALLY

Home economists and health professionals constantly urge everyone to replace processed or refined foods with more natural foodstuffs. "Fiber" has become a household word. In the search for vitamin-packed foods which are high in fiber content, the versatile squash stands high on the list.

Summer squash, the dieter's delight, offers a mere five calories per ounce while being generous with vitamins A and C, along with iron, calcium, part of the B complex, niacin, riboflavin, and thiamine. Combining summer squash with cheese or milk naturally boosts protein and calcium levels.

Not to be outdone, winter squash also is high in nutrient value. A small serving provides enough vitamin A to satisfy the recommended daily requirement. Those nutrient bonuses attributed to summer squash also are present in winter squash.

For the sake of good dietary practices, think about using squash along with other fibrous and nutritious food. Since summer squash has a tender, edible skin and seeds which contain cellulose, this is an excellent source of unabsorbable roughage.

Recipes combining all kinds of squash with rice, bran, bulgur, barley, corn, and dried beans are found in the chapters VEGETABLE DISHES, BREADS & BUTTERS, and SALADS.

Preparing squash with low cholesterol commercial products is an example of dietary wisdom. "Cholesterol-free" or "light" products can be substituted in any recipe calling for eggs and dairy products. Instead of whole milk or cream, use skim milk. For browning, substitute a low-fat olive-oil spray. Replace sour cream with yogurt. Cream cheese may be replaced by Neufchâtel or a low-fat cream cheese.

Sauté in olive oil or white wine instead of butter or margarine. The alcohol burns away in just a few minutes. Simmer chopped vegetables in chicken or beef broth until tender crisp, avoiding fat completely.

Steam fresh vegetables instead of frying them. This is one healthful way to promote fat-free cooking. Eat summer squash raw as you do carrots, cauliflower, and cucumbers. There is room for tender, sliced summer squash in any tossed or layered salad.

For a salt-free diet, check the Seasonings Chart in the chapter COOKING SQUASH. Use recommended herbs as salt substitutes.

There is no better way to practice preventative medicine than by indulging in good nutrition. Squash all dietary bad habits and shop, garden, cook, and eat intelligently for a healthier tomorrow.

CHAPTER 2

THE SQUASH HARVEST

CANNING

Since a boiling water bath is only suitable for high acid fruits and vegetables, namely tomatoes (which actually are a fruit), we cannot use this basic canning method for either summer or winter squash.

Squash pickles are the exception because of the vinegar (high acid) content. So unless you already have a pressure cooker or intend to acquire one which may be used for processing canned vegetables, your squash crop belongs in the freezer with all other low acid produce. You may wish to dry some when the freezer is full.

Zucchini, cocozelle, crookneck, and all other summer varieties may be pressure canned using either a raw pack or hot pack method. In either case, the squash should be carefully washed and sliced.

Raw pack: Sterilize pint or quart glass jars. Pack squash tightly. Pour in boiling water to within ½ inch of jar top, making sure all squash is covered. Add ½ teaspoon salt per pint and fasten lids firmly. Seal and process in a pressure cooker at 10 pounds pressure for 25 minutes for pints, 30 minutes for quarts.

Hot pack: Wash and slice squash. Cover with water to which salt has been added. Bring to a rolling boil and remove from heat. Drain and reserve liquid. Pack squash in hot sterilized pint or quart glass jars, filling to within ½ inch of top with reserved cooking liquid. Seal and process in a pressure cooker at 10 pounds pressure for 30 minutes for pints, 40 minutes for quarts.

Winter squash and pumpkins.
Winter squash and pumpkins may be cubed or mashed for canning. Since most recipes call for mashed pulp, it seems logical to can it in this state. However, if time is short at processing time and there is no shortage of jars, cubing the vegetable is a shorter process and, therefore, may be preferable. Both types of preparation are adaptable to hot pack canning.

Cubed: Cut squash or pumpkin into one-inch cubes after removing seeds and stringy portion. Pare. Place in large pot or kettle, adding boiling water to cover. Allow liquid to resume a rolling boil. Drain vegetable, reserving liquid. Fill hot sterilized pint or quart glass jars with hot vegetable, fill to within ½ inch with hot reserved liquid. Add ½ teaspoon salt per pint. Seal and process in a pressure cooker at 10 pounds pressure for 60 minutes for pints, 80 minutes for quarts.

Mashed: Cut vegetable into several pieces. Remove seeds and stringy portion. Steam, boil, or bake at 350° F. until pulp is soft. Remove skin and mash. Stir over very low heat until thoroughly heated. Pack to within ½ inch of jar top. Seal and process in a pressure cooker at 10 pounds pressure for 60 minutes for pints, 80 minutes for quarts.

Storage of canned goods.
What a beautiful and satisfying sight—shelf after shelf lined with colorful jars of home-canned produce! Cucurbits, in their many varieties and diverse forms, can make many nutritious mainstays. Stews, casseroles, soups, and lots of other dishes created from the canned ingredients-in-waiting will please many a hungry soul in the months to come.

Assuming care and precision have been the watchwords of the canning process, that only suitable and perfect equipment (especially jars and lids) has been used, then only proper storage conditions are needed to make the products of your own canning factory a total economic and gastronomic success.

Summer squash, because of a high water content, becomes very soggy when it is canned or frozen. For this reason, the cook may prefer to preserve summer varieties by grating the vegetable for use in bread recipes or processing it into puree for use in soups. Frozen supplies of squash prepared in this manner are very welcome and very useful during those months when fresh summer squash is scarce and/or expensive in the marketplace.

Grated or julienned in a food processor, summer squash may be frozen in large quantities. Drain squash prepared in this manner by putting it into a colander and covering it with a flat plate or lid. Weight the lid with something heavy and allow squash to drain for several hours. Pack squash in containers of convenient size, such as one-pint freezer bags which store easily. Grated squash may be used in breads, soups, frittatas, and other recipes in which cooked squash is included.

Puree may consist of solely squash or a combination of squash, other vegetables, and seasonings. See pages 87-91 in the chapter VEGETABLE DISHES for suggestions.

FREEZING

All squash, both summer and winter, must be blanched prior to freezing. This involves heating the vegetable in either boiling water or steam for a sufficient amount of time to stop enzyme action or the ripening process. To blanch, place sliced or cubed squash in a wire basket or sieve and lower into boiling water. As soon as the water reaches a rolling boil, covering all of the squash, begin timing. When the time is up, lift the basket from the water, allowing it to drain, and immediately put the blanched squash into a large bowl of ice water. Fill basket with more squash while waiting for blanching water to return to a boil. Submerge basket and begin process all over again. Squash should remain in cold water bath for the same amount of time that it was submerged in boiling water. Once a blanching-cooling-draining-packing routine is established on a production line basis, you quickly become very efficient in preparing produce for the freezer.

When the squash has cooled, drain it well, pack into suitable containers, label, and stack your winter supply of beautiful vegetables in your freezer. Squash keeps well, although most authorities suggest that everything within a freezer, regardless of keeping qualities, should have at least an annual turnover.

Summer squash. Slice and blanch all summer squash for 3 minutes. A cooling period of 3 minutes also is required. Pack in freezer containers leaving at least ½-inch headroom to allow for expansion. Seal and freeze.

Winter squash. Winter squash adapts well to winter storage in the cellar or in a garage that has protection from freezing temperatures. For this reason, few people devote any precious freezer space to these vegetables. If space is no issue, however, winter squash may be cubed or sliced and steam blanched, cooled, and packed. If preferred, winter squash and pumpkin may be precooked until tender, mashed, and the pulp frozen. In either case, cut pumpkin or squash into manageable pieces. Scoop out seeds and stringy portions. Cook until blanched or steam until flesh is soft. Remove skin, mash pulp, cool, and pack. *Note:* Spaghetti squash may be frozen whole. Simply blanch in boiling water for 10-12 minutes. Immerse in ice water the same length of time. Then slip it into a plastic bag, or wrap in aluminum foil and place in the freezer. To thaw, expose squash to room temperature for 50-60 minutes. Boil whole for 30-45 minutes depending upon size.

Freezer containers. Containers of various sizes and descriptions are available commercially. Square containers waste the least amount of space in freezers. Wide-mouth canning jars also accommodate frozen produce; the wide opening is designed to facilitate the removal of still frozen food. Freezer bags are also available, including the heat-seal variety in which the food may be cooked in boiling water. An at-home sealing mechanism is commercially available.

Frugality often promotes the use of recycled dairy containers, such as those for quarts and half-gallons of milk or 8- and 16-ounce cartons of cottage cheese, yogurt, etc. Recycled coffee cans, used alone or lined with plastic bags and sealed with their own plastic lids, make useful freezer containers, holding approximately 3½ cups of frozen food per 1-pound can.

All packages should be airtight. Freezer bags must be squeezed to expel all air. Their tops should be twisted, doubled back, and fastened securely with wire or rubber bands. Recycled dairy and coffee containers should be taped at the opening with freezer or masking tape, which then can be labeled with an indelible pen.

COOKING FROZEN FOOD

Most cooks overextend their cooking enthusiasm and cook vegetables too long. This reduces nutritional value. Flavor, texture, and appearance are also victims of overcooking.

Frozen squash is best prepared without gradual thawing. For every pint of frozen squash, heat ½ cup of salted water to a rolling boil. Add squash; allow boiling to resume. Reduce heat and gently simmer for 10 minutes. If squash has been frozen in cooking bags, simply immerse bag into boiling water, reduce heat, and simmer as above, allowing 3-5 minutes of additional cooking time.

See the chapter VEGETABLE DISHES for squash combinations suitable for freezing.

DRYING

One of the oldest methods of preserving garden, orchard, and berry patch produce is drying. If you are weary of canning or have run out of jars and the freezer is bulging, why not dry some of the surplus squash?

The drying process is a time-consuming one, too much so for some of its detractors. There is only one way to discover whether drying has any merits from your perspective and that is to try it, at least on a small scale, and make your own decision whether to try this preserving method again.

Squash is one of several vegetables which adapt to the drying process. Perhaps an experiment in drying surplus zucchini will convince you of certain economical advantages which you may apply later to other homegrown produce. Onions, peppers, carrots, and beans also may be preserved in this manner. So too can many fruits, such as plums, apples, grapes, and apricots, which are expensive when bought at the supermarket.

Dryers are available commercially in houseware stores and health food stores. Articles on the drying process appear frequently in gardening magazines. All this indicates an ever-widening interest in drying fruits and vegetables at home.

In primitive times, drying was accomplished by using the only dryer available—the sun. Solar drying is possible today in geographical areas where the heat is intense enough, the air is dry enough, and the individuals involved have sufficient patience.

A bed sheet spread out in a sunny spot is all that is needed for equipment. If it can be spread over an old window screen and suspended or supported enough to allow for bottom air circulation, so much the better. The racked, drying vegetables must be brought inside at sunset since nighttime moisture would defeat your purpose. More elaborate drying systems call for the use of specially constructed trays, designed to fit your oven, or independent drying boxes either of the homemade or purchased variety. Directions for construction and use of such equipment can be obtained by writing to the Office of Information, U.S. Department of Agriculture, Washington, DC 20250, requesting Bulletin 984, *Farm and Home Drying of Fruits and Vegetables.*

Pumpkin was preserved in pioneer homes simply by cutting it into chunks and stringing it to hang with other vegetables, fruits, and even meats to dry over the wood stove. Since squash does not lend itself to drying as easily as other garden produce, today we slice both squash and pumpkin and steam blanch them for 6-8 minutes. Some prefer to shred these vegetables for faster drying because dried squash does adapt best to recipes in which it is mashed.

Squash and pumpkin may be dried on racks in an oven set at 140°F. The oven door should be left ajar to allow for some air circulation. Cheesecloth spread over oven racks may suffice, although more suitable equipment is easily constructed.

The drying process is a lengthy one; an infinite supply of patience is recommended. When the vegetables finally become brittle, they should be removed from the oven or dryer and conditioned for several days. In a large nonmetal crock, glass jar, or plastic container, allow dried material to condition in a well-ventilated room for a week or more. Stir vegetables each day. Cover container with netting or cheesecloth to avoid attracting insects. As a final precaution against spoilage, oven pasteurization is highly recommended. Spread dried squash or pumpkin on racks; preheat to 175°F. and give vegetables a 10-minute exposure to this heat. Cool completely, pack in glass jars and seal and store in a cool dry place.

STORING SQUASH

Zucchini, cocozelle, crookneck, and all other related summer squash must be canned, frozen, or dried as they cannot be winter-stored successfully.

Winter squash and all other tough-skinned varieties keep well when stored properly in cool, dry areas, such as basements, root cellars, attics, and some garages. The ideal temperature is between 45°-60°F., pumpkins somewhat cooler at 35°-40°F. No cucurbit can survive extended exposure to below-freezing temperatures.

All squash and pumpkins should be handled gently for they bruise and dent easily. Such wounds encourage spoilage in even the healthiest of specimens.

It is tempting, when caught in the garden without a knife, to simply tug away at a squash, wrenching it stemless from the umbilical vine, but for maximum storage condition, cut squash and pumpkin from the vine, retaining a stem of at least one inch in length. Use a sharp knife. Allow your storage crop to cure outdoors in a sunny spot for about two weeks. Cured in this manner, your cucurbits may

be packed off to the storage area to be placed on shelves in single layers and not touching, or wrapped individually in newspaper and stacked in crates or baskets. They then will last most of the winter.

TOO MUCH SQUASH

To use as much of an abundant squash harvest as possible, think about new ways of incorporating this versatile vegetable in other favorite recipes. Simply add it to baked custard and decrease milk one-half cup for each cup of squash. Substitute cooked, mashed squash for potatoes in potato bread recipes. Combine zucchini with bran cereals to make baked products. Use squash with dried beans for soups. Tuck chopped zucchini into standard recipes for tuna, ham, and potato salad. Combine summer squash with pasta for stick-to-the-ribs meals.

There truly is no such thing as too much squash. For variations which may not have been included in other recipes, rely on Zucchini Bingo (see page 25) to prove new ways of preparing the very prolific varieties of summer squash.

CHAPTER 3

COOKING SQUASH

The word squash is a derivative of *askútasquash*, an Indian word meaning "raw or uncooked." Summer squash can, indeed, be eaten raw. Winter squash, however, because of the density of its flesh and toughness of its skin, needs to spend some time with the stove to become palatable. Only the Tahitian Melon is mentioned for uncooked consumption.

The skin and seeds of summer squash, when picked at the proper size, should be very tender, making it unnecessary to peel or seed the vegetable. Winter squash, on the other hand, has very tough skin and well-developed seeds which must be removed. Directions for cooking both types under a variety of circumstances are enumerated in the following lists. Familiarity with these cooking steps should make it possible to convert microwave recipes into conventional cookery and conventional recipes into those suitable for microwaving procedures.

HOW TO COOK SUMMER SQUASH

There is no need to pare or remove seeds if the squash is young.

1. Steam whole, cut in half, diced, sliced, or cubed. This is the best way to cook tender crisp squash.
2. Blanch whole, cut in half, diced, sliced, or cubed.
3. Butter-steam sliced, diced, cubed, or grated, covered over high heat. Watch!
4. Simmer whole, cut in half lengthwise, diced, sliced (rounds or strips), or cubed in boiling salted water.
5. Sauté in margarine or oil diced, sliced, cubed, grated, or halved, until squash is barely tender.

6. Halve lengthwise; scoop out pulp and combine with stuffing mixture. Bake 25-30 minutes at 350°F.

7. Steam, blanch, or simmer whole until almost tender. Slice in half lengthwise and scoop out pulp. Combine with cooked ingredients for filling. Bake in a little water for 10 minutes at 375°F.

8. For deep-fat frying, heat fat 360°-375°F. Cut squash into strips or rounds, dredge in flour or tempura batter, and fry until golden.

9. For stir-frying, heat oil in a wok and stir strips or slices 2-3 minutes until tender crisp. Stir-frying preserves flavor and nutrients.

10. Bake, thinly sliced, in a baking dish with other ingredients at 350ºF.

11. Microwave on HIGH for 3 or 4 minutes per pound.

HOW TO COOK WINTER SQUASH

The first four methods are useful for filling or stuffing the smaller winter squash, such as acorn, butternut, and buttercup.

1. Cut in half lengthwise, remove seeds, and place halves cut side down on a baking sheet. Bake in a preheated 350°F. oven for 45 minutes. Turn cut side up, loosen squash pulp, and add cooked filling, or remove pulp, mash, and combine with cooked filling. Return to oven 15 minutes more.

2. Place cut side up, fill, and bake in a 350°F. oven for 1 hour.

3. Puncture squash. Place whole in a baking pan with ¼ inch water. Bake until skin starts to give. Remove from oven and cut in half lengthwise. Remove seeds and stringy portion. Return to pan cut side up. Fill and bake until done.

4. Boil whole and cut in half lengthwise. Remove seeds and stringy portion. Loosen pulp a little, season, and stuff. Reheat if necessary.

5. Peel with a swivel vegetable peeler, cut into small chunks or slices, and sauté or fry.

6. Microwave: Cut squash in half lengthwise. Discard seeds and fiber. Place squash cut side down in a microsafe baking dish. Cover with plastic wrap. Microwave on HIGH for 4 minutes. Turn squash over and rotate dish. Microwave on HIGH for 4 more minutes until squash is fork tender but still firm.

The following methods are helpful for large squashes which are tedious to peel or difficult to cut.

7. Wrap squash in plastic wrap or wax paper and microwave on HIGH for 2 minutes. Allow squash to stand several minutes, and then cut in half for further cooking or chunk it up for a specific recipe.

8. In the absence of a microwave, use a heavy knife or cleaver with the help of a mallet, if necessary, to cut the squash if it is too large to cook whole.

9. Boil whole, cut into chunks, and peel to eat as is or mash.

10. Boil large chunks, peel, and mash in a blender, mixer, or food processor.

11. Cut into large chunks. Place skin side up in a shallow baking pan. Bake at 375°F.

12. Puncture squash and bake whole at 350°F. until skin begins to give.

100,000 VARIETIES
ZUCCHINI
BINGO

To start, sauté in a 10-inch skillet, 1 cup zucchini, sliced, and 1 medium onion, sliced, in 2 tablespoons margarine. Now make a selection from each category to make a prize-winning dish, e.g., B-3, I-9, N-5, G-1, O-8.

B

Vegetables
1 cup, chopped

1. Peas, celery
2. Tomatoes, mushrooms
3. Tomatoes, eggplant
4. Summer squash, celery
5. Tomatoes, corn
6. Tomatoes, green peppers
7. Green peppers, carrots, celery
8. Peas, mushrooms
9. Green peppers, celery
10. Green peppers, mushrooms

I

Meat
½ pound, cooked

1. Chicken, chopped
2. Ground lamb
3. Turkey, chopped
4. Ground pork
5. Tuna
6. Ham, chopped
7. Bacon, crumbled
8. Ground beef
9. Ground veal
10. Ground pork sausage or Italian sausage

N

Sauces
1 cup

1. Béchamel
2. Fresh tomato
3. Tomatoes-cheese
4. Sour cream
5. Sour cream-tomato
6. Chicken Veloute
7. Cheese
8. Mornay
9. Custard
10. Mayonnaise

G

Bottom
1 cup, cooked

1. Vegetable squash
2. Rice
3. Barley
4. Noodles
5. Macaroni
6. Spaghetti
7. Spinach noodles
8. Use acorn squash shells
9. Use baking dish
10. Use scooped out zucchini shells

O

Top
½ cup

1. Bread crumbs
2. Bread crumbs, cheese
3. Crushed potato chips
4. Cracker crumbs
5. Grated Swiss
6. Grated Parmesan
7. Grated Romano
8. Grated Mozzarella
9. Grated Cheddar
10. Grated Gruyère

**BAKE AT 350° F. ABOUT 30 MINUTES.
SERVES 2-4**

SEASONINGS CHART

Zucchini and ...	Basil	Black Pepper	Cayanne Pepper	Celery Seed	Chives	Cumin	Curry	Dill Seed	Garlic	Ginger	Hot Pepper	Lemon
Beef	X	X	X	X	X	X	X		X	X	X	X
Chicken		X			X		X	X	X	X	X	X
Fish	X	X			X		X	X	X	X		X
Ham												X
Lamb	X	X				X	X	X	X	X		X
Pork	X	X	X		X				X	X	X	
Sausage		X							X		X	
Veal	X	X									X	X
Beets				X				X		X		X
Cabbage		X		X					X			
Carrots		X		X						X		X
Cauliflower	X							X				X
Celery		X			X							X
Corn	X	X	X	X	X					X		
Cucumber	X	X	X	X	X			X				
Eggplant	X	X				X						X
Garbanzos	X	X							X		X	
Green Beans	X	X	X					X	X	X		X
Green Peppers	X	X			X				X		X	X
Onions	X	X	X	X	X		X	X	X			
Mushrooms	X	X	X									X
Peas		X	X	X					X			
Spinach	X	X	X									
Tomatoes	X	X			X	X	X		X	X		
Eggs	X	X	X	X	X							
Cheese	X		X	X	X			X			X	
Noodles or Rice	X	X		X	X						X	
Mayo or Sour Cream		X						X				X
Tomato Sauce	X					X			X		X	
White Sauce			X				X					X

The chart lists possible flavorings that you may find helpful in creating your own recipes. Add about one-eighth of a teaspoon of any one or a mixture of the suggested seasonings and correct, if needed, according to your personal preferences. What you like is what is right.

Mint	Mustard Seed	Nutmeg	Onion	Oregano	Paprika	Parsley	Prepared Mustard	Rosemary	Sage	Savory	Sesame Seed	Tarragon	Thyme	White Pepper
X	X	X	X	X	X	X	X	X		X	X	X	X	
		X			X	X		X	X			X	X	X
		X			X	X	X					X	X	X
	X	X					X	X						
X	X		X	X	X	X		X			X		X	
	X	X		X	X	X		X	X	X	X	X	X	
	X	X	X		X	X	X		X	X			X	
		X		X			X	X				X	X	X
X		X						X						
			X	X	X									X
X		X				X					X		X	
		X		X	X			X		X	X	X		X
X	X				X					X	X		X	X
	X		X	X		X					X			
X	X		X		X			X						
				X		X		X					X	
			X	X		X		X						
X		X	X				X				X	X	X	
	X		X	X							X	X	X	
	X	X	X	X										X
	X		X	X	X							X		
X		X	X							X	X			
	X	X		X			X				X			X
	X	X	X			X						X		X
		X				X		X			X	X		X
		X		X		X	X	X		X			X	X
		X		X		X								
X			X			X						X		X
		X		X		X								
X		X				X					X	X		X

THE SAUCE RECIPES

1. **Béchamel**
   2 tablespoons margarine
   2 tablespoons all-purpose
     flour
   1 cup warm milk

   Melt margarine (stove top or microwave).
   Stir in flour and heat for 30 seconds or more.
   Stir in warm milk and cook until thick and bubbly.

2. **Fresh Tomato**
   ½ cup minced onions
   3 tablespoons olive oil
   2 pounds tomatoes, peeled, seeded, and chopped
   1 clove garlic, minced
   1 bay leaf
   1 teaspoon each oregano, parsley, marjoram, and sugar

   Sauté onions in oil until soft. Add remaining ingredients.
   Simmer until thick and reduced.

3. **Tomato-Cheese**
   1 cup shredded sharp cheese
   ½ can condensed tomato soup, undiluted
   1 tablespoon tomato paste
   ½ cup milk

Heat first three ingredients until cheese is melted.
Stir in milk.

4. **Sour Cream**
   ½ cup sour cream
   1 cup condensed cream soup (chicken, shrimp, or mushroom), undiluted

   Combine all ingredients.

5. **Sour Cream-Tomato**
   ½ cup sour cream
   ¾ cup tomato puree
   ½ teaspoon paprika

   Combine all ingredients.

6. **Chicken Velouté**
   2 tablespoons margarine
   2 tablespoons all-purpose flour
   1 cup chicken broth
   1 egg yolk, beaten with cream (optional)
   sherry (optional)

   Make as for béchamel. Add last two ingredients for a richer sauce.

7. **Cheese**
   1 cup milk
   2 tablespoons butter
   2 tablespoons all-purpose flour
   2 tablespoons grated cheddar cheese

On stove top or in microwave, heat milk for 2 minutes. Melt butter for 2 minutes in microwave or add to milk on stove top and heat until melted.
Combine flour with milk and butter until well blended and cook until boiling. Add cheese and blend.

8. **Mornay**
   2 tablespoons margarine
   2 tablespoons all-purpose flour
   1 cup cream
   1 egg yolk, slightly beaten
   Parmesan cheese, grated

   Make as for béchamel. Stir in egg yolk and Parmesan cheese.

9. **Mayonnaise**
   ¾ cup shredded sharp cheese
   ¼ cup chopped onions
   1 tablespoon lemon juice
   ½ cup low-calorie mayonnaise
   salt to taste
   chervil to taste

   Combine all ingredients.

10. **Custard**
    2 eggs, lightly beaten
    1½ cups milk

    Mix together.

CHAPTER 4

APPETIZERS & SNACKS

ANTIPASTO

The Italians have a habit of serving delicious and imaginative tidbits as appetizers or an antipasto, meaning "before food." The only problem with this custom is that all of the components of the antipasto are so good and so filling that you can get carried away with trying a dab of everything and forget that dinner is yet to come!

Ordinarily, antipasto consists of several cold meats, selections of cheese, and vegetables, marinated or raw, of all descriptions.

The zucchini, in various marinades, makes a very appropriate antipasto contribution.

ZUCCHINI AND CAULIFLOWER À LA GRECQUE

5-6   **SMALL ZUCCHINI**
1   **MEDIUM HEAD CAULIFLOWER**
1   **MEDIUM GREEN PEPPER**
½   **CUP OLIVE OIL**
1   **CUP LEMON JUICE**
2   **LEMON SLICES**
1   **TEASPOON SALT**
1   **CLOVE GARLIC, CRUSHED**
½   **TEASPOON COARSELY GROUND BLACK PEPPER**
1   **TEASPOON DRIED THYME**
¼   **TEASPOON HOT PEPPER SAUCE**

Slice zucchini, break cauliflower into florets, julienne the green pepper.

Combine all other ingredients in a large saucepan. Bring to a boil, add vegetables. Reduce heat and simmer until tender but not mushy.

Place in a large bowl or crock, cover, and refrigerate. Serve cold. *Note:* Other ingredients may be combined with the zucchini: green beans, Brussels sprouts, carrots, eggplant, onions, mushrooms, artichoke hearts, cherry tomatoes, small whole beets, red kidney beans, garbanzos, etc.

PREPARATION TIME: 10 MINUTES
COOKING TIME: 4 MINUTES
SERVES: 6

DILLED ZUCCHINI

2   **MEDIUM ZUCCHINI**
  WATER
  SALT
  OLIVE OIL OR MELTED MARGARINE
  DILL SEED OR DILL WEED TO TASTE

Cut zucchini lengthwise enough times to make sticks. In a medium saucepan, cover with boiling water to which salt has been added and simmer for 2-3 minutes until tender crisp. Drain well.

Drizzle with oil or melted margarine. Sprinkle with dill seed or dill weed. Chill.

PREPARATION TIME: 10 MINUTES
COOKING TIME: 2-3 MINUTES
SERVES: 6

ZUCCHINI VINAIGRETTE

¼ CUP DRY SHERRY OR VERMOUTH
1 ENVELOPE ITALIAN DRESSING MIX
½ CUP OLIVE OIL
¼ CUP WHITE VINEGAR
3 TABLESPOONS CHOPPED CHIVES
3 TABLESPOONS CHOPPED SWEET
   PICKLES
2 TABLESPOONS CHOPPED FRESH
   PARSLEY
3 TABLESPOONS CHOPPED GREEN
   PEPPERS
4 SMALL-MEDIUM ZUCCHINI, GOLDEN
   ZUCCHINI, OR OTHER SUMMER
   SQUASH
   WATER

In a small mixing bowl, combine the first eight ingredients and mix thoroughly.

Slice zucchini lengthwise in sticks of appropriate size. Place in a large saucepan of water, bring to a boil, and simmer about 4 minutes until tender crisp. Drain well. Pat dry with paper towels.

Arrange zucchini sticks in a large shallow dish. Pour marinade over them. Cover and chill overnight. Spoon marinade over sticks occasionally. Serve cold.

PREPARATION TIME: 10 MINUTES
COOKING TIME: 4 MINUTES
SERVES: 4

ZUCCHINI ROUNDS

1 MEDIUM ZUCCHINI OR OTHER
   SUMMER SQUASH
1 3-OUNCE PACKAGE CREAM CHEESE
1 TABLESPOON CHOPPED GREEN
   ONIONS, TOPS INCLUDED
2 TEASPOONS CHOPPED FRESH
   PARSLEY
1 TEASPOON SOUR CREAM
½ TEASPOON WHITE VINEGAR

Peel zucchini with potato peeler. Use end of peeler to core the zucchini, removing seed section.

In a small mixing bowl, combine all other ingredients and stuff zucchini with this mixture. Slice and serve chilled.

PREPARATION TIME: 15 MINUTES
SERVES: 4

CANAPÉS

A canapé, another French standby, is a snack or appetizer consisting of delectable tidbits spread or layered upon a small piece of toast or bread. Canapés are usually more substantial, a bit fancier, and somewhat more formal than the typical hors d'oeuvre. A tray full of elaborately prepared canapés is, indeed, a sight to see.

Substituting zucchini slices for toast or bread rounds is another example of how to cut calories and yet serve tasty and decorative appetizers.

ZUCCHINI CANAPÉS

**ZUCCHINI OR OTHER SUMMER
    SQUASH
SALT
TUNA FISH SALAD
HAM SALAD
HARD-BOILED EGG SLICES, TOPPED
    WITH A ROLLED ANCHOVY
CREAM CHEESE AND MINCED
    CLAMS**

Small zucchini or other summer squash may be sliced in rounds ¼ inch thick. Salt, then drain on paper towels. Top with any of the other ingredients and serve as snacks.

PREPARATION TIME: 10 MINUTES
SERVES: VARIABLE

ZUCCHINI-WALNUT SPREAD

1   **CUP GRATED AND DRAINED
     ZUCCHINI**
1   **CUP GRATED SHARP CHEDDAR
     CHEESE**
¾   **CUP LOW-CALORIE MAYONNAISE**
½   **CUP CHOPPED WALNUTS**
1   **TEASPOON LEMON JUICE**

In a small mixing bowl, combine all ingredients. Refrigerate for several hours. Serve with crackers or bite-sized raw vegetables.

PREPARATION TIME: 10 MINUTES
MAKES: 2 CUPS

WINTER SQUASH CHEESE SPREAD

1   **MEDIUM ACORN, HUBBARD, OR**
      TURBAN SQUASH
      WATER
1   **8-OUNCE PACKAGE CREAM CHEESE**
¼ **CUP BUTTER**
¼ **CUP CHOPPED PITTED DATES**
2   **TABLESPOONS DRAINED AND**
      CHOPPED CHUTNEY
      PARTY-SIZE BREAD

Cut a one-inch slice from bottom of squash. Remove stem end and discard seeds. Set squash in a saucepan with one inch of boiling water. Reduce heat, cover, and simmer until squash is tender, about 20 minutes. Shell should remain firm. Do not overcook. Transfer squash to colander and cool.

Beat together room-temperature cream cheese and butter. Mix in the dates and chutney.

Remove squash flesh allowing a shell ¼ inch thick to remain. Combine flesh with cream cheese mixture and spoon into shell. Cover squash and chill. Serve spread with bread slices.

PREPARATION TIME: 15 MINUTES
COOKING TIME: 20 MINUTES
SERVES: 8-12

PUMPKIN CIDER BOWL

1   **5- OR 6-POUND EDIBLE PUMPKIN**
      WATER
      MARGARINE
½ **CUP SUGAR OR HONEY**
½ **CUP APPLE CIDER**
1   **CINNAMON STICK**
¼ **TEASPOON GROUND NUTMEG**

Preheat oven to 350°F. Cut lid from pumpkin. Scoop out seeds and stringy portion. Score interior several times. Place pumpkin and lid upside down in a large shallow pan. Add ¼-inch water and place in a preheated oven. Reduce heat to 300°F. and bake 30 minutes. Remove from oven and rub interior with margarine. Allow to cool.

In a small saucepan, heat remaining ingredients until sugar or honey is dissolved. Pour mixture into pumpkin and reheat until pumpkin is done. Serve from the "cider bowl" by scooping out the cider-laced pulp. Greater amounts of cider may be used and served as a drink; the pulp eaten later.

PREPARATION TIME: 20 MINUTES
BAKING TIME: 30 MINUTES
SERVES: 6-8

HORS D'OEUVRES

The French, with their hors d'oeuvres meaning "outside of the essential part of the meal," are very imaginative in preparing appetizers. Strips or rounds of summer squash served with tasty dips make delicious and nutritious hors d'oeuvres. Such appetizers as raw squash, served singly or in combination with other raw vegetables, provide you and your guests with the beginnings of a wholesome diet. How much more nutritious and less caloric than the grease-laden potato chip.

ZUCCHINI STICKS

Cut young, tender squash into strips of appropriate size for dunking.
Serve with seasoned salt and/or one or more of the following cocktail dips:

SIMPLE CURRY DIP

1   CUP LOW-FAT PLAIN
     YOGURT
1   TABLESPOON CURRY
     POWDER

Mix well and serve. Makes 1 cup.

BLUE CHEESE DIP

1   3-OUNCE PACKAGE
     CREAM CHEESE
1   OUNCE CRUMBLED
     BLUE CHEESE OR
     ROQUEFORT
2   TEASPOONS CHILI
     SAUCE
½   TEASPOON PAPRIKA
½   TEASPOON
     WORCESTERSHIRE
     SAUCE
¼   TEASPOON SALT
     PINCH FRESHLY
     GROUND WHITE
     PEPPER

Blend well and serve. Makes 1 cup.

COTTAGE CHEESE DIP

1   12-OUNCE CARTON
     CREAM-STYLE
     COTTAGE CHEESE
1   TABLESPOON CHOPPED
     FRESH CHIVES
½   TEASPOON HOT
     PEPPER SAUCE

Blend well and serve. Makes 1½ cups.

CRAB AND ZUCCHINI APPETIZERS

4   SMALL ZUCCHINI
¼   CUP CHOPPED GREEN PEPPERS
1½   TABLESPOONS MARGARINE
1   TABLESPOON ALL-PURPOSE FLOUR
¼   CUP MILK
¼   CUP CHOPPED GREEN ONIONS
¼   TEASPOON PAPRIKA
⅛   TEASPOON SALT
⅛   TEASPOON FRESHLY GROUND
       BLACK PEPPER
3   DASHES TABASCO SAUCE
1   6-OUNCE CAN CRABMEAT, DRAINED

Slice zucchini into ¾-inch rounds. Scoop out half of each round. Reserved pulp may be saved for other use.

Combine green peppers and margarine in a medium baking dish. Microwave on HIGH for 2 minutes. Add flour and milk, blending until smooth. Add green onions and seasonings. Microwave until thick, about 1 minute. Stir in crabmeat.

Fill each squash cup with crab mixture. Microwave on HIGH stuffed squash in two batches for 2 minutes at a time.

PREPARATION TIME: 15 MINUTES
COOKING TIME: 5 MINUTES
SERVES: 20

ZUCCHINI TART APPETIZER

     COOKING SPRAY
¾   CUP GRATED PARMESAN CHEESE
2   TABLESPOONS DRY WHOLE-WHEAT
       BREAD CRUMBS
3   EGGS
½   CUP WHOLE-WHEAT FLOUR
2   CUPS HALF-AND-HALF
2   TEASPOONS SALT
     RED PEPPER
1   MEDIUM ZUCCHINI, CHOPPED
¼   CUP CHOPPED RED BELL PEPPERS
2   TABLESPOONS CHOPPED FRESH
       PARSLEY

Preheat oven to 375°F. Grease a 9-inch pie pan or flan pan with cooking spray. Combine ¼ cup Parmesan cheese and bread crumbs using this to coat baking pan, shaking excess into a separate container.

In a small mixing bowl, beat eggs and combine with flour. Add milk and seasonings and mix well. In a separate bowl, combine vegetables, parsley, and egg mixture and mix thoroughly.

Pour mixture into the pan and bake until filling is firm and an inserted knife comes out clean. Cool on a wire rack. Cut into serving sizes and serve while still warm.

PREPARATION TIME: 10 MINUTES
BAKING TIME: 20 MINUTES
SERVES: 12

ZUCCHINI APPETIZERS

4   SMALL ZUCCHINI, THINLY SLICED
1   CUP BISCUIT MIX
½   CUP CHOPPED ONIONS
⅓   CUP GRATED PARMESAN CHEESE
½   TEASPOON SALT
     PEPPER TO TASTE
6   CLOVES GARLIC, MINCED
½   CUP VEGETABLE OIL
4   EGGS, BEATEN
2   LARGE TOMATOES, CHOPPED

Preheat oven to 350°F. In a large mixing bowl, mix ingredients and spread in a 13 x 9 x 2-inch baking pan. Bake 25 minutes, or until golden. Cut into squares.

PREPARATION TIME: 15 MINUTES
BAKING TIME: 25 MINUTES
SERVES: 12-16

LOW-CALORIE PIZZA

24   SLICES SUMMER SQUASH, CUT ½
     INCH THICK
⅔   CUP SPAGHETTI SAUCE
2   OUNCES GRATED LOW-FAT
     MOZZARELLA CHEESE
2   OUNCES GRATED PARMESAN
     CHEESE
¼   TEASPOON DRIED OREGANO
¼   TEASPOON FRESHLY GROUND
     BLACK PEPPER
24   SLICES FRESH MUSHROOMS
24   SLICES RIPE OLIVES
     PAPRIKA TO TASTE

Prepare sliced vegetables. Drain squash slices on paper towels. Place drained squash slices on well-greased baking sheet.

In a medium mixing bowl, combine next five ingredients and spoon mixture onto each slice of squash. Top each with a mushroom and olive slice. Sprinkle with paprika.

Broil slices until heated and serve while hot.

PREPARATION TIME: 15 MINUTES
COOKING TIME: 5 MINUTES
MAKES: 24

ZUCCHINI CHEESE SQUARES

3 CUPS THINLY SLICED ZUCCHINI
1 CUP BISCUIT MIX
½ CUP CHOPPED ONIONS
½ CUP GRATED PARMESAN CHEESE
2 TABLESPOONS CHOPPED FRESH
    PARSLEY
1 TEASPOON SEASONED SALT
½ TEASPOON DRIED OREGANO
    PEPPER TO TASTE
1 CLOVE GARLIC, CHOPPED
½ CUP VEGETABLE OR OLIVE OIL
4 EGGS, BEATEN

Preheat oven to 350°F. Grease a 13 x 9 x 2-inch baking pan. In a large mixing bowl, combine ingredients and spread in the pan. Bake until golden, about 25 minutes. Cut into squares.

PREPARATION TIME: 10 MINUTES
BAKING TIME: 25 MINUTES
MAKES: ABOUT 48

SANDWICHES

Carrying the canapé idea a bit further, more substantial offerings in the form of bona fide sandwiches are also possible, using large slices of summer squash. The variety of possible sandwich fillings is limited only by one's imagination and taste preferences. Here are some possibilities.

ZUCCHINIWICHES

ZUCCHINI
TUNA, HAM, OR CHICKEN SALAD
PIMIENTO, SMOKY, OR ROQUEFORT
    CREAM CHEESE
DEVILED EGG SALAD
PAPRIKA

Slice zucchini (about 2½-3 inches in diameter) into ¼-inch rounds. Spread one slice of zucchini with a mixture such as one of the seven suggestions. Top with another slice. Sprinkle with paprika. Serve with soup or as an appetizer.

PREPARATION TIME: 5 MINUTES
SERVES: VARIABLE

ZUCCHINI-PEANUT BUTTER SANDWICH

2 CUPS GRATED AND DRAINED
   ZUCCHINI
1 CUP GRATED CARROTS
¼ CUP CHOPPED CELERY
⅓ CUP LOW-CALORIE MAYONNAISE
⅓ CUP PEANUT BUTTER
8 SLICES CRACKED WHEAT BREAD
   LETTUCE LEAVES

In a medium mixing bowl, combine zucchini with carrots, celery, and mayonnaise. Spread peanut butter on four bread slices. Top with vegetable mixture and lettuce leaf. Complete sandwich by adding bread slice spread with additional mayonnaise, if desired.

PREPARATION TIME: 25 MINUTES
SERVES: 4

SQUASH SANDWICH

1 MEDIUM ZUCCHINI OR OTHER
   SUMMER SQUASH
1 4½-OUNCE CAN DEVILED HAM
1 TEASPOON HORSERADISH
8 SLICES PUMPERNICKEL OR DARK
   RYE BREAD
4 TABLESPOONS LOW-CALORIE
   MAYONNAISE, YOGURT, OR
   COTTAGE CHEESE
   SEASONED SALT

Slice squash as thinly as possible. In a small mixing bowl, mix deviled ham and horseradish and spread on four slices of bread.

In a separate bowl, mix other ingredients and spread on remaining pieces of bread. Layer on reserved squash slices and top with deviled ham-horseradish bread slices. Cut sandwiches and serve.

PREPARATION TIME: 15 MINUTES
SERVES: 4

SEED SNACKS

Seeds of the cucurbit family are definitely edible. They can be toasted or baked. After toasting or baking, an additional step is all that is necessary to prepare them for nibbling. That step is to crack the seeds so that the shells may be removed. See recipes on page 40.

Food value of seeds. Plant protein is found in greatest concentration in seeds. Analogous to the egg of the animal world, a well-known source of protein, squash and pumpkin seeds are also storehouses of nutritious food elements.

PUMPKIN SEED BALLS

PUMPKIN SEEDS
SUNFLOWER SEEDS
SESAME SEEDS
WHEAT GERM, TOASTED
PUMPKIN SEED BUTTER (SEE
    CHAPTER 12)
PEANUT BUTTER

Prepare seeds as for toasted or baked. Mix with remaining ingredients. Add salt, if needed. Shape into tiny balls.

PREPARATION TIME: VARIABLE
SERVES: VARIABLE

CURRIED TOASTED SEEDS

¼ CUP PEANUT OR SAFFLOWER OIL
2 TEASPOONS CURRY POWDER
1 TEASPOON WORCESTERSHIRE
    SAUCE
2 DROPS HOT PEPPER SAUCE
PUMPKIN OR SQUASH SEEDS

Preheat oven to 350°F. In a small saucepan, heat mixture of oil and seasonings. Stir in seeds. Line a baking sheet with aluminum foil. Spread seeds on the sheet and bake until crisp. Crack the seeds, remove the shells, and serve.

PREPARATION TIME: 20 MINUTES
BAKING TIME: VARIABLE
SERVES: VARIABLE

TOASTED SEED SNACKS

SQUASH OR PUMPKIN SEEDS
WATER
SAFFLOWER OR PEANUT OIL
SALT

Preheat oven to 250°F. Seeds from squash or pumpkin first should be separated from fibers. In a medium saucepan, cover seeds with boiling water to which salt has been added. Reduce heat and simmer gently for 1½-2 hours.

Spread seeds on a baking sheet. Using a pastry brush, coat with safflower or peanut oil. Salt generously. Bake in a slow oven until adequately browned and crunchy, about 45 minutes.

Crack the seeds, remove the shells, and serve.

```
PREPARATION TIME: 20 MINUTES
COOKING TIME: 1½-2 HOURS
BAKING TIME: 45 MINUTES
SERVES: VARIABLE
```

BAKED SEED SNACKS

SQUASH OR PUMPKIN SEEDS
SALT
WATER

Preheat oven to 300°F. Separate squash or pumpkin seeds from fibrous material. Soak seeds *overnight* in a mixture of 2 teaspoons salt per 1 cup water.

Drain on paper towels. Place on a baking sheet and bake 30-45 minutes. Do not allow to brown.

Crack the seeds, remove the shells, and serve.

```
PREPARATION TIME: 10 MINUTES
BAKING TIME: 30-45 MINUTES
SERVES: VARIABLE
```

SNACK CHIPS

Winter squash and pumpkin, not to be entirely outdone by their summer cousins in the snack category, lend themselves to a recipe for a hot appetizer or snack. Some people prefer a sweeter taste, in which case sugar may be substituted for the garlic salt.

SQUASH/PUMPKIN SNACK CHIPS

½ **POUND WINTER SQUASH OR**
  PUMPKIN
  ICE WATER
  OIL FOR COOKING
½ **TEASPOON GARLIC SALT**
1½ **TABLESPOONS CURRY POWDER**

Peel and seed squash or pumpkin. Slice as thin as possible into potato chip size. Place in the refrigerator to *chill for 45 minutes* in a large bowl of ice water. Drain well. Dry with paper towels.

Deep-fry until browned. Sprinkle with combined seasonings.

PREPARATION TIME. 1 HOUR
COOKING TIME: 5 MINUTES
SERVES: VARIABLE

TAHITIAN SQUASH CHIPS

1 **TAHITIAN MELON SQUASH**

Preheat oven to 250ºF. Cut portions of squash into 1/4-inch strips. Remove peeling. Place strips on a baking sheet and bake for 3-4 hours. This sweet winter squash will taste like apricots but has fewer calories.

PREPARATION TIME: 10 MINUTES
BAKING TIME: 3-4 HOURS
SERVES: VARIABLE

CHAPTER 5
SALADS

Green and yellow summer squash, if they are small and tender, make both colorful and tasty contributions to salad dishes. The dieter, concerned about calorie consumption, can munch away happily on raw vegetables without experiencing any guilt.

Salad dressings, both homemade and commercial, come in such variety that salads of all descriptions and flavors may be served very frequently without fear of boring any palate. Experimenting with additions of mustard seed, dill seed, celery seed, sesame seed, parsley, garlic, or onion salt also will add interest and your own personal touch.

Main-dish salads, using almost everything in the garden, can substitute for more expensive entrées which must be purchased at the market. A zucchini niçoise, for example, makes a mighty filling meal, with or without the optional tuna fish.

ZUCCHINI NIÇOISE

¾ **CUP OLIVE OIL**
¼ **CUP RED WINE VINEGAR**
¼ **TEASPOON SALT**
⅛ **TEASPOON COARSELY GROUND BLACK PEPPER**
4 **MEDIUM POTATOES, BOILED, PEELED, AND SLICED**
½ **POUND GREEN BEANS**
5 **CUPS SLICED ZUCCHINI**
2 **MEDIUM ONIONS, SLICED LEAF LETTUCE**
1 **6½-OUNCE CAN TUNA**
2 **MEDIUM TOMATOES, QUARTERED**
2 **HARD-BOILED EGGS, QUARTERED**

In a small mixing bowl, make a salad dressing by combining olive oil, vinegar, and seasonings.

Place potato slices in a large shallow bowl and marinate in some of the dressing. Chill.

Cut beans into 2-inch pieces and boil in salted water in a small saucepan for 15 minutes until tender crisp. Drain, marinate, and chill.

Slice zucchini into very thin slices. Marinate and chill. Slice, marinate, and chill onions.

Line a salad bowl or serving dish with fresh, crisp lettuce leaves. If tuna is to be included, center it in the serving dish, surrounding it with mounds of marinated vegetables. Garnish with tomato and egg wedges. Flavors are enhanced by preparing marinated vegetables several days in advance.

PREPARATION TIME: 35 MINUTES
COOKING TIME: 15 MINUTES
SERVES: 4

SQUASH SALAD PIE

1   3-OUNCE PACKAGE LIME
    GELATIN
1   CUP BOILING WATER
1   CUP APPLESAUCE OR PINEAPPLE
    SAUCE
2   TABLESPOONS LEMON JUICE
1   CUP JULIENNED ZUCCHINI OR
    OTHER SUMMER SQUASH
½   CUP MINCED CARROTS
2   TABLESPOONS MINCED GREEN
    ONIONS
1   CUP DRAINED SMALL CURD
    COTTAGE CHEESE
1   TEASPOON MINCED LEMON PEEL
    SALT TO TASTE
    FRESH BASIL LEAVES
    (OPTIONAL)
    FRESH PARSLEY, MINCED
    (OPTIONAL)

In a large mixing bowl, add gelatin to boiling water. Add fruit sauce and lemon juice. Place in the refrigerator until slightly jelled.

Fold in the vegetables and pour into a well-greased 9-inch pie pan. Return to the refrigerator until mixture is firm.

In a medium mixing bowl, combine remaining ingredients except herbs and spread onto pie mixture. Garnish with fresh basil leaves or minced parsley, if desired.

PREPARATION TIME: 2 HOURS 30 MINUTES
SERVES: 6

ZUCCHINI-MACARONI SALAD

2 CUPS DICED SMALL ZUCCHINI
3 CUPS COOKED SHELL MACARONI
2 CUPS SHREDDED CABBAGE
1 CUP SHREDDED CARROTS
½ CUP CHOPPED GREEN PEPPERS
½ CUP SLICED RED RADISHES
3 TABLESPOONS MINCED ONIONS
1 CUP LOW-CALORIE MAYONNAISE
   OR SOUR CREAM
2 TABLESPOONS LEMON JUICE
1½ TEASPOONS SUGAR
1½ TEASPOONS DRY MUSTARD
1 TEASPOON SALT
   DILL SEED
   LEAF LETTUCE

Do not peel tender young squash. In a large bowl, combine the first twelve ingredients. Mix well. Sprinkle with dill seed. Serve chilled on fresh, crisp lettuce leaves.

PREPARATION TIME: 30 MINUTES
SERVES: 6

ZUCCHINI-AVOCADO SALAD

6 SMALL ZUCCHINI
   WATER
2 AVOCADOS, PEELED AND DICED
1 SMALL ONION, MINCED
¼ CUP OLIVE OIL
1 TABLESPOON RED WINE
   VINEGAR
1 CLOVE GARLIC, MINCED
1½ TEASPOONS SALT
¼ TEASPOON FRESHLY GROUND
   BLACK PEPPER
   LEAF LETTUCE
   TOMATO WEDGES

Cut zucchini in half lengthwise. Blanch in boiling salted water 5 minutes. Scoop out pulp and drain shells upside down. Dice zucchini pulp. Combine with avocado and onion in a large mixing bowl.

In a small mixing bowl, combine oil, vinegar, garlic, salt, and pepper. Mix well. Pour dressing into squash mixture. Spoon into shells and chill thoroughly.

Serve on fresh, crisp lettuce leaves. Garnish with tomato wedges.

PREPARATION TIME: 20 MINUTES
COOKING TIME: 5 MINUTES
SERVES: 6-8

ZUCCHINI SLAW

1   **MEDIUM ZUCCHINI, JULIENNED**
1   **MEDIUM CARROT, JULIENNED**
1   **STALK CELERY, CHOPPED**
½   **MEDIUM GREEN PEPPER, CHOPPED**
½   **SMALL HEAD WHITE OR RED CABBAGE, GRATED**

DRESSING:

⅓   **CUP OLIVE OIL**
2   **TABLESPOONS LEMON JUICE**
1   **TEASPOON DIJON MUSTARD**
    SALT AND PEPPER TO TASTE

Toss chilled vegetables in a large bowl. In a small mixing bowl, whisk *Dressing* ingredients together and pour over vegetables.

PREPARATION TIME: 20 MINUTES

SERVES: 2

ZUCCHINI-TOMATO ASPIC RING

2   **ENVELOPES UNFLAVORED GELATIN**
½   **CUP COLD WATER**
4   **CUPS TOMATO JUICE**
1   **TABLESPOON LEMON JUICE**
2   **TEASPOONS GRATED ONIONS**
1   **TEASPOON DRIED BASIL**
1   **CUP THINLY SLICED ZUCCHINI**
1   **CUP DICED ZUCCHINI**
½   **CUP DICED GREEN PEPPERS**
½   **CUP SLICED GREEN OLIVES**
    COTTAGE CHEESE
    PAPRIKA

In a small mixing bowl, soften gelatin in cold water. In a small saucepan, heat tomato juice. Add gelatin and stir until dissolved. Add seasonings and mix well. Allow to cool.

Cover bottom of a well-greased ring mold with ¼ inch layer of gelatin mixture. Place mold in the refrigerator and chill until gelatin is set.

Place a layer of zucchini slices on top of molded gelatin. Layer with ¼ inch liquid gelatin, chill, and allow to set.

In a large mixing bowl, combine remaining vegetable ingredients. Stir in remaining gelatin. Mix well and pour into mold. Chill, unmold, and fill ring cavity with cottage cheese, if desired. Sprinkle cottage cheese with paprika.

PREPARATION TIME: 2 HOURS

SERVES: 8

ZUCCHINI SALAD BOWL

2 **SMALL ZUCCHINI, THINLY SLICED**
2 **CUPS COOKED DICED POTATOES**
1 **CUP COOKED PEAS**
1 **CUP COOKED DICED CARROTS**
½ **CUP CHOPPED ONIONS**
¾ **CUP SOUR CREAM OR LOW-CALORIE MAYONNAISE**
1 **TABLESPOON DICED SWEET PICKLE**
2 **TABLESPOONS WHITE VINEGAR**
½ **TEASPOON SALT**
⅛ **TEASPOON FRESHLY GROUND BLACK PEPPER**
LEAF LETTUCE

Cut zucchini into very thin slices, or quarter lengthwise and dice, if preferred. In a large bowl, combine with all other ingredients except lettuce and toss lightly. Chill. Serve on fresh, crisp lettuce leaves.

PREPARATION TIME: 30 MINUTES
SERVES: 4

ZUCCHINI-SALMON MOUSSE

2 **ENVELOPES UNFLAVORED GELATIN**
4 **TABLESPOONS COLD WATER**
½ **CUP BOILING WATER**
½ **CUP SLICED ZUCCHINI**
½ **CUP LOW-CALORIE MAYONNAISE**
1 **TABLESPOON LEMON JUICE**
1 **TEASPOON SALT**
HOT PEPPER SAUCE
2 **CUPS DRAINED SALMON OR TUNA**
½ **CUP MINCED ZUCCHINI**
½ **CUP WHIPPING CREAM**
TOMATO WEDGES
FRESH PARSLEY

If available, use a fish-shaped mold. Otherwise, either a solid or ring mold is suitable. In a large mixing bowl, soften gelatin in the cold water. Add the boiling water and stir until gelatin is dissolved. Allow mixture to cool.

Pour ¼-inch layer of gelatin into the mold and chill until set, then layer zucchini slices on top.

Add mayonnaise, lemon juice, salt, and hot pepper sauce to remaining gelatin mixture. Chill until thick but not yet firm. Add flaked fish and minced zucchini. Beat well.

Whip cream and fold into fish mixture. Spoon into mold. Chill until firm. Unmold on platter and garnish with tomato wedges and fresh parsley.

PREPARATION TIME: 1 HOUR 30 MINUTES
SERVES: 4-6

ZUCCHINI SALAD RUSSE

2 CUPS DICED AND DRAINED
    ZUCCHINI
1 CUP COOKED DICED TURNIPS
1 CUP COOKED DICED POTATOES
1 CUP COOKED DICED BEETS
1 CUP COOKED PEAS
    FRENCH DRESSING
    LOW-CALORIE MAYONNAISE
    LEAF LETTUCE OR SPINACH
    HARD-BOILED EGGS,
      QUARTERED (OPTIONAL)
    TOMATO WEDGES (OPTIONAL)

In a large mixing bowl, combine all vegetables and marinate in French dressing for several hours.

Before serving, add enough mayonnaise to bind mixture together. Layer a serving platter with fresh, crisp lettuce or spinach leaves. Mound salad in the center and garnish with hard-boiled eggs and/or tomato wedges.

PREPARATION TIME: 30 MINUTES
SERVES: 8

ZUCCHINI BEAN SALAD

½ POUND DRIED KIDNEY OR PINTO
    BEANS
4 CUPS WATER
2 CUPS TORN SPINACH
1 SMALL ZUCCHINI, THINLY
    SLICED
1 CUP CHOPPED ONIONS
1 CUP CUBED SWISS CHEESE
½ CUP LOW-CALORIE MAYONNAISE
2 TABLESPOONS WHITE VINEGAR
    OR SWEET PICKLE JUICE
1 TABLESPOON LEMON JUICE
2 TABLESPOONS GRATED ONIONS
1 TABLESPOON DIJON MUSTARD
½ TEASPOON SALT
¼ TEASPOON FRESHLY GROUND
    BLACK PEPPER

Rinse beans. In a large saucepan, bring the beans to a boil in the water. Simmer until beans are tender but not overcooked, about 1 hour 15 minutes. The texture should be firm. Drain beans.

In a large mixing bowl, combine with the spinach, zucchini, chopped onions, and cheese. In a small mixing bowl, make a sauce of the remaining ingredients and stir into the spinach mixture. Chill.

PREPARATION TIME: 20 MINUTES
COOKING TIME: 1 HOUR 15 MINUTES
SERVES: 6

SPAGHETTI SQUASH SALAD

1   **SPAGHETTI SQUASH**
    WATER
4   **CARROTS**
2   **GREEN ONIONS**
½   **CUP OIL AND VINEGAR**
    COMBINED OR BOTTLED
    ITALIAN DRESSING

Cut squash in half lengthwise. Discard seeds. Place halves, cut side up in a large skillet. Add ½-inch water and bring to a boil. Reduce heat and simmer, covered, for 20 minutes.

Scrape carrots and place in the skillet with the squash. Continue to cook until carrots are tender crisp, about 10 minutes. Drain vegetables, remove from skillet, and allow to cool.

Trim onions and slice lengthwise into narrow strips. Slice cooked carrots into matchstick strips. Using a fork, fluff up spaghetti-like strands of squash and transfer to a bowl. Add onions, carrots, and dressing and toss. Cover salad and refrigerate. Toss again before serving.

PREPARATION TIME: 15 MINUTES
COOKING TIME: 30 MINUTES
SERVES: 3

ZUCCHINI SALAD DRESSING

2   **CUPS ZUCCHINI, CUT INTO**
    MATCHSTICK STRIPS
½   **CUP LOW-FAT PLAIN YOGURT**
¼   **CUP SOUR CREAM**
1   **TEASPOON DILL WEED**
    SALT AND PEPPER TO TASTE

In a glass or plastic storage container, mix ingredients and use for salad dressing.

PREPARATION TIME: 10 MINUTES
MAKES: 2 CUPS

CHAPTER 6

CASSEROLES

SQUASHES WITH MEAT AND FISH

Actually, a casserole is the container in which a meal is cooked and frequently served rather than the recipe or concoction itself. Many of us, under harried conditions, have expressed gratitude to whatever genius invented the casserole. That "genius" was the first prehistoric human who devised a vessel in which to cook whatever was available. The modern-day cook, appreciative of the time- and effort-saving practice of preparing an entire meal in a single pot, has many utensils from which to choose, ranging from the old faithful cast-iron Dutch oven to the automatic slow cooker.

Members of the versatile squash family combined with other vegetables, cheeses, meats, herbs, and spices can produce many tasty one-dish meals.

ZUCCHINI STROGANOFF

½ **POUND GROUND BEEF**
¼ **CUP CHOPPED ONIONS**
½ **CAN CONDENSED CREAM OF MUSHROOM SOUP, UNDILUTED**
1 **CUP UNCOOKED EGG NOODLES**
1 **CUP SLICED ZUCCHINI SEASONED SALT AND PEPPER**
½ **TEASPOON DRIED CHERVIL OR BASIL**
⅔ **CUP SOUR CREAM**

Place ground beef and onions in a 10-inch skillet. Cook until beef loses pink color.

Spread over beef mixture the mushroom soup, noodles, zucchini, and seasonings. Simmer covered until the noodles are done.

Stir in sour cream and warm through. *Note:* Try other ground meats such as pork sausage (marjoram or savory), lamb (basil or oregano), or veal (rosemary or tarragon).

PREPARATION TIME: 10 MINUTES
COOKING TIME: 15 MINUTES
SERVES: 2

ZUCCHINI-BARBECUED CHICKEN

2 **MEDIUM ZUCCHINI, CUT INTO ¼-INCH SLICES**
2 **CHICKEN BREASTS, BONED SALT AND PEPPER TO TASTE**
⅔ **CUP BARBECUE SAUCE**
½ **TEASPOON DRIED OREGANO**
½ **TEASPOON DRIED BASIL**
¼ **CUP CHOPPED ONIONS**
2 **TEASPOONS SHERRY**

Preheat oven to 375°F. Place zucchini in bottom of shallow 1 ½-quart greased baking pan. Arrange chicken over zucchini.

Combine remaining ingredients and pour over chicken. Bake, covered, for 1 hour, basting every 15 minutes with the liquid.

PREPARATION TIME: 15 MINUTES
BAKING TIME: 1 HOUR
SERVES: 2-3

ZUCCHINI-LAMB PILAF

2 POUNDS LAMB, CUT INTO 1-INCH
    CUBES
1 CUP DICED ONIONS
1 TABLESPOON OLIVE OIL
2 TABLESPOONS MARGARINE
2 TEASPOONS TOMATO PASTE
1 TEASPOON DRIED THYME
    SALT AND PEPPER TO TASTE
1 CUP WATER (OR BROTH)
3 CUPS DICED ZUCCHINI
1 CUP DICED YELLOW SUMMER
    SQUASH
1½ CUPS DICED CARROTS
1 CUP DICED ONIONS
1 15-OUNCE CAN GARBANZO
    BEANS, DRAINED
    RICE, COOKED

In a large skillet, brown meat and sauté onions in olive oil and margarine.

Add tomato paste, seasonings, water or broth, and vegetables. Simmer 30-40 minutes until meat and vegetables are tender. Serve over hot buttered rice.

> PREPARATION TIME: 15 MINUTES
> COOKING TIME: 30-40 MINUTES
> SERVES: 6

ZUCCHINI-BEEF CASSEROLE

1½ POUNDS SHOULDER STEAK, CUT
    INTO STRIPS
1 MEDIUM ONION, CHOPPED
½ TEASPOON SALT
1 8-OUNCE CAN TOMATO SAUCE
1 4-OUNCE CAN MUSHROOM
    PIECES WITH JUICE
1 8-OUNCE CAN WATER
5 CUPS ZUCCHINI, CUT INTO
    CHUNKS
8 OUNCES MONTEREY JACK OR
    SWISS CHEESE, CUT INTO
    SLICES

Brown steak in a large skillet. Add onion. Sauté 2 minutes. Add salt, tomato sauce, mushrooms, and water. Simmer until tender about 1½ hours.

Add zucchini for 15 minutes. Top with cheese and cover until cheese melts.

> PREPARATION TIME: 15 MINUTES
> COOKING TIME: 2 HOURS
> SERVES: 6-8

ZUCCHINI-GROUND BEEF ITALIAN

½ CUP CHOPPED ONIONS
1 MEDIUM GREEN PEPPER,
    CHOPPED
1 CLOVE GARLIC, MINCED
1 TABLESPOON OLIVE OIL
½ POUND GROUND BEEF
1 CUP THINLY SLICED ZUCCHINI
1 CUP TOMATOES, PEELED,
    SEEDED, AND CHOPPED
½ TEASPOON DRIED OREGANO
½ TEASPOON DRIED BASIL
    DASH HOT PEPPER SAUCE
    SALT AND PEPPER TO TASTE

Preheat oven to 350°F. In a large saucepan, sauté onions, green pepper, and garlic for 2 minutes in olive oil. Stir in ground beef. Cook until browned.

Stir in remaining ingredients. Turn into a 1-quart casserole. Bake for 30 minutes.

PREPARATION TIME: 15 MINUTES
BAKING TIME: 30 MINUTES
SERVES: 2

ZUCCHINI-HAM DELIGHT

3 CUPS THINLY SLICED ZUCCHINI
    WATER
2½ TABLESPOONS ALL-PURPOSE
    FLOUR
2 TABLESPOONS MELTED
    MARGARINE
1 CUP MILK
½ CUP SHREDDED CHEDDAR
    CHEESE
1-2 CUPS COOKED CHOPPED HAM
1 MEDIUM ONION, SLICED
    SALT AND PEPPER TO TASTE
1 CUP BREAD CRUMBS, MIXED
    WITH 3 TABLESPOONS
    MELTED MARGARINE
¼ CUP GRATED PARMESAN
    CHEESE

Preheat oven to 350°F. In a medium saucepan, cook zucchini in boiling salted water about 5 minutes. Drain.

In a large saucepan, add flour to margarine and stir in milk and cheese. Cook until thick and add ham.

Place zucchini in bottom of shallow 1½-quart well-greased baking dish. Arrange onion rings over zucchini. Salt and pepper. Spoon cheese sauce over vegetables. Mix crumbs with the Parmesan cheese and sprinkle over the top. Bake about 20 minutes.

PREPARATION TIME: 15 MINUTES
BAKING TIME: 20 MINUTES
SERVES: 4

SPAGHETTI ZUCCHINI

1½ **POUNDS ITALIAN SAUSAGE,
      THINLY SLICED**
2   **MEDIUM GREEN PEPPERS,
      MINCED**
1   **CUP MINCED ONIONS**
1   **CLOVE GARLIC, MINCED**
3   **MEDIUM ZUCCHINI, SHREDDED**
2   **CUPS PEELED AND CHOPPED
      TOMATOES**
½   **CUP CHOPPED JALAPEÑO
      PEPPERS**
1   **TEASPOON DRIED BASIL**
1   **TEASPOON CHILI POWDER**
½   **TEASPOON SALT**
1   **TEASPOON LEMON JUICE**
½   **TEASPOON TABASCO SAUCE**
½   **CUP GRATED PARMESAN
      CHEESE**
      **COOKED SPAGHETTI TO SERVE
      EIGHT**

Cook sausage, green peppers, onions, and garlic in a large skillet coated with cooking spray. When meat is lightly browned, drain mixture.

Add the next eight ingredients and simmer for 15 minutes, until zucchini is tender. Remove from heat, add cheese, and mix well. Serve over hot pasta.

PREPARATION TIME: 20 MINUTES
COOKING TIME: 15 MINUTES
SERVES: 8

ZUCCHINI AND TUNA

3 TABLESPOONS MARGARINE
1 CUP SHREDDED AND DRAINED
   ZUCCHINI
½ CUP CHOPPED GREEN PEPPERS
½ CUP SLICED CELERY
⅓ CUP CHOPPED ONIONS
1 CAN TUNA, DRAINED
2 TABLESPOONS ALL-PURPOSE
   FLOUR
1 CUP MILK
2 TABLESPOONS DRIED PARSLEY
½ CUP GRATED CHEDDAR CHEESE
1 TEASPOON SALT
½ TEASPOON DRIED DILL WEED
6 OUNCES EGG NOODLES, COOKED
   CRACKER CRUMBS

Preheat oven to 325°F. In a large saucepan, melt margarine. Stir in zucchini, green peppers, celery, and onions. Cook until soft.

Blend in the next seven ingredients until thick. Add cooked noodles. Place in a 1-quart casserole. Sprinkle with crumbs. Bake until heated through, about 15 minutes.

PREPARATION TIME: 30 MINUTES
BAKING TIME: 15 MINUTES
SERVES: 2-3

ZUCCHINI-LAMB SHANK PROVENÇALE

2 CLOVES GARLIC, SLIVERED
6 LAMB SHANKS
2 TABLESPOONS VEGETABLE OIL
3 MEDIUM ONIONS, DICED
2 CUPS PEELED AND DRAINED
   TOMATOES
3 TEASPOONS SALT
1 BAY LEAF
½ CUP WATER OR DRY RED WINE
3 MEDIUM ZUCCHINI, SLICED

Preheat oven to 350°F. Insert garlic slivers into lamb shanks. In a Dutch oven, brown meat in oil.

Add onions and cook until soft. Pour off excess fat. Add tomatoes, seasonings, and liquid. Bake uncovered for 1 hour 30 minutes.

Add zucchini and mix well. Add more water if necessary and continue to bake 30 minutes more.

PREPARATION TIME: 15 MINUTES
BAKING TIME: 2 HOURS
SERVES: 6

ZUCCHINI-MEAT LOAF RATATOUILLE

⅓ CUP OLIVE OIL
2 CLOVES GARLIC, MINCED
1 CUP CHOPPED ONIONS
3 MEDIUM ZUCCHINI, SLICED
3 SMALL GREEN OR SWEET RED
    PEPPERS, CUT INTO STRIPS
1 MEDIUM EGGPLANT, THINLY
    SLICED
1 TABLESPOON DRIED OREGANO
3 TABLESPOONS ALL-PURPOSE
    FLOUR
    SALT AND PEPPER TO TASTE
2 CUPS TOMATOES, PEELED,
    SEEDED, AND CHOPPED
    LEFTOVER MEAT LOAF SLICES
3 SLICES LOW-FAT MOZZARELLA
    CHEESE

Preheat oven to 350°F. In a large skillet, heat olive oil. Add garlic and onions. Sauté until onions are transparent.

In a large bowl, toss zucchini, peppers, eggplant, oregano, flour, salt, and pepper until well combined. Add this mixture to the skillet, topping with the tomatoes. Cover and cook over low heat 1 hour. Uncover and continue cooking until very thick, about 15 minutes more.

In a 1 ½-quart casserole, start with a layer of the zucchini mixture then add a slice of meat loaf and continue until casserole is filled. Top with mozzarella cheese. Heat thoroughly in oven about 10 minutes. *Note:* This dish is good hot or cold and makes an excellent omelette filling with or without the meat loaf.

PREPARATION TIME: 20 MINUTES
COOKING TIME: 1 HOUR 25 MINUTES
SERVES: 4

ZUCCHINI-CHICKEN HUNGARIAN

1½ POUNDS CHICKEN PIECES *OR*
    1 POUND COOKED CHICKEN
    MEAT
¾ CUP SEASONED FLOUR
½ CUP MARGARINE
¼ CUP VEGETABLE OIL
2 CUPS ZUCCHINI, CUT INTO ½-
    INCH SLICES
1 TABLESPOON LEMON JUICE
1 TABLESPOON HUNGARIAN
    PAPRIKA
4 OUNCES EGG NOODLES,
    UNCOOKED
½ CUP SOUR CREAM

Coat chicken pieces with seasoned flour. Melt ¼ cup margarine and the oil in a large skillet. Sauté chicken until tender. (If using cooked chicken meat, place in a baking dish to warm in a low oven.)

In a large saucepan, melt the remaining margarine and cook the zucchini, lemon juice, and paprika 8-10 minutes.

Cook noodles. Drain and combine with zucchini. Blend in half the sour cream. Place in a greased, 1 ½-quart casserole with chicken. Top with remaining sour cream. Heat through, about 10 minutes:

PREPARATION TIME: 35-40 MINUTES
COOKING TIME: 20 MINUTES
SERVES: 2-3

BUTTERNUT-LAMB DELUXE

5 CUPS BAKED BUTTERNUT
    SQUASH
½ CUP CHOPPED ONIONS
½ POUND GROUND LAMB
¼ CUP TOMATO SAUCE
¼ TEASPOON GROUND NUTMEG
2 TABLESPOONS MARGARINE
2 TABLESPOONS ALL-PURPOSE
    FLOUR
1 CUP MILK
½ CUP GRATED LOW-FAT
    MOZZARELLA CHEESE
    BREAD CRUMBS

Preheat oven to 325°F. Scoop out flesh from butternut. Cook onions and lamb in a medium skillet until pink color is gone. Add tomato sauce and nutmeg.

In a large saucepan, melt margarine. Add flour and stir in milk and cheese until thick.

Add lamb mixture and squash. Sprinkle bread crumbs on the bottom of a shallow, well-greased 1-quart baking dish. Spread squash mixture evenly and top with more crumbs. Bake about 20 minutes. *Note:* For extra consistency and richness, stir into cooked squash ⅓ cup more bread crumbs.

PREPARATION TIME: 30 MINUTES
BAKING TIME: 20 MINUTES
SERVES: 4

ZUCCHINI MOUSSAKA

2 POUNDS GROUND BEEF
1 LARGE ONION, CHOPPED
1 CLOVE GARLIC, MINCED
3 MEDIUM TOMATOES, DICED
½ CUP CHILI SAUCE
2 TEASPOONS SALT
¼ TEASPOON FRESHLY GROUND
   BLACK PEPPER
¼ TEASPOON GROUND ALLSPICE
¼ TEASPOON GROUND CINNAMON
½ POUND MONTEREY JACK
   CHEESE, SHREDDED
8 CUPS ZUCCHINI, SLICED ¼ INCH
   THICK
1 TABLESPOON VEGETABLE OIL

Preheat oven to 350°F. Cook ground beef, onion, and garlic in a Dutch oven until meat is lightly browned and onion is tender. Add tomatoes, chili sauce, and seasonings. Bring mixture to a boil. Reduce heat and simmer for 45 minutes.

Remove from heat and set aside. Stir in half of cheese. Cook zucchini until tender crisp in hot oil.

In an 8-inch baking dish, place a layer of zucchini, top with a layer of meat mixture, repeat layering ending with zucchini and sprinkle with remaining cheese. Bake 25 minutes. Serve hot. Recipe may be doubled and surplus frozen.

PREPARATION TIME: 20 MINUTES
COOKING TIME: 45 MINUTES
BAKING TIME: 25 MINUTES
SERVES: 8

ZUCCHINI-VEAL CUTLET ESPAÑA

6 VEAL CUTLETS
1 EGG, BEATEN
¾ CUP DRY BREAD CRUMBS
¼ CUP OLIVE OIL
2 CUPS PEELED AND SLICED
   TOMATOES
1½ TEASPOONS SALT
⅓ TEASPOON DRIED OREGANO
   SALT AND PEPPER TO TASTE
   PARMESAN CHEESE, GRATED
3 MEDIUM ZUCCHINI

Dip veal into beaten egg and dredge in crumbs. In a large skillet, brown lightly in olive oil.

Layer meat with tomatoes, seasonings, and cheese. Cover mixture and simmer 30 minutes. Cut zucchini into ¼-inch slices and place over veal-tomato mixture. Simmer 25-30 minutes more.

PREPARATION TIME: 10 MINUTES
COOKING TIME: 1 HOUR
SERVES: 6

WINTER SQUASH STUFFED WITH STEW

4 ACORN SQUASH
  WATER
2 TABLESPOONS MELTED BUTTER
2 TABLESPOONS MAPLE SYRUP
½ CUP CHOPPED ONIONS
1 POUND LEAN PORK, CUBED
2 TABLESPOONS VEGETABLE OIL
¼ TEASPOON FRESHLY GROUND
  BLACK PEPPER
¼ TEASPOON DRIED MARJORAM
1 CLOVE GARLIC, MINCED
1 CUP PEELED AND CHOPPED
  TOMATOES
2 TABLESPOONS ALL-PURPOSE
  FLOUR
1½ CUPS BEEF CONSOMMÉ
2 MEDIUM CARROTS, PEELED AND
  SLICED INTO ROUNDS
2 MEDIUM ONIONS, PEELED AND
  QUARTERED
  WATER
1½ CUPS PEAS OR 10-OUNCE
  FROZEN PACKAGE PEAS

Preheat oven to 350°F. Remove tops or "lids" from squash and set aside. Scoop out seeds. Place squash in boiling, salted water and parboil for 8 minutes. Drain and turn upside down on paper towels. Brush interior of squash with melted butter and syrup. Place squash cups and lids in a baking pan with ½ inch of water. Bake for 20 minutes or longer, until tender.

In a large skillet, brown onions and pork in oil and stir in seasonings and tomatoes. Sprinkle meat mixture with flour, mix well, and add consommé. Cover stew and simmer until meat is tender.

In a medium saucepan, cook carrots and onions in boiling water, add peas, and simmer until all vegetables are tender. Drain.

Combine vegetables and meat mixture. Fill squash with this hot stew. Place lids on top and serve.

PREPARATION TIME: 20 MINUTES
BAKING TIME: 20 MINUTES
SERVES: 4

ZUCCHINI SOLE CASSEROLE

1   POUND FILLET OF SOLE
1   TABLESPOON LEMON JUICE
½   TABLESPOON SALT
2   MEDIUM ZUCCHINI, SLICED
      ¼ INCH THICK
½   CUP CHOPPED GREEN PEPPERS
¼   CUP CHOPPED ONIONS
1   TABLESPOON BUTTER
1   11-OUNCE CAN CONDENSED
      CREAM OF MUSHROOM SOUP,
      UNDILUTED
2   TABLESPOONS WHITE WINE
1   TABLESPOON CHOPPED FRESH
      PARSLEY
½   TEASPOON FRESH DILL WEED

Preheat oven to 350°F. Sprinkle fish with lemon juice and salt. Slice fillet in half and roll up. Place in a shallow baking dish.

In a large saucepan, sauté zucchini, peppers, and onions in butter. Simmer until liquid is evaporated. Add soup, wine, parsley, and dill weed. Heat to boiling point and pour over fillet. Bake about 15 to 20 minutes, or until fish flakes. Do not overcook.

PREPARATION TIME: 25 MINUTES
BAKING TIME: 20 MINUTES
SERVES: 4

ZUCCHINI-SAUSAGE COMBO

1   POUND BULK PORK SAUSAGE
1   TEASPOON MINCED ONIONS
2   MEDIUM ZUCCHINI, SLICED
      WATER
½   CUP DRY BREAD CRUMBS
½   CUP MILK
½   CUP GRATED AMERICAN CHEESE
½   CUP COOKED MIXED
      VEGETABLES
¼   TEASPOON DRIED OREGANO
¼   TEASPOON DRIED PARSLEY
¼   TEASPOON DRIED SAVORY
¼   TEASPOON CELERY SEED OR
      MUSTARD SEED
2   EGGS, BEATEN

Preheat oven to 325°F. In a large skillet, crumble sausage. Add onions and cook slowly until pork is lightly browned. Remove excess fat.

In a small saucepan, simmer zucchini in salted water until barely tender. Drain and add to meat along with bread crumbs, milk, cheese, vegetables, and seasonings. Stir eggs in slowly. Pour into a 1 ½-quart well-greased casserole. Bake 30 minutes.

PREPARATION TIME: 15 MINUTES
BAKING TIME: 30 MINUTES
SERVES: 4

BUTTERNUT-TURKEY CASSEROLE

1 **BUTTERNUT SQUASH (2 POUNDS)**
¾ **CUP MINCED ONIONS**
2 **TABLESPOONS MARGARINE**
2 **CUPS TOASTED CROUTONS**
½ **TEASPOON POULTRY SEASONING**
½ **TEASPOON SALT**
PEPPER TO TASTE
1 **CUP CHICKEN BROTH**
2 **CUPS COOKED DICED TURKEY OR CHICKEN**
½ **CUP SHREDDED CHEDDAR CHEESE**

Preheat oven to 350ºF. Cut squash in half lengthwise and discard seeds. Bake, cut side down, in a baking pan for 50-60 minutes until squash is tender. Scoop out pulp and mash.

Sauté onions in margarine. Add toasted croutons and seasonings. Add broth, mashed squash, and turkey. Place mixture in a 1½-quart well-greased casserole. Bake for 20 minutes. Sprinkle cheese on top and return to oven until cheese is melted.

PREPARATION TIME: 25 MINUTES
BAKING TIME: 1 HOUR 20 MINUTES TOTAL
SERVES: 6

ZUCCHINI-COQ AU VIN

6 **CUPS SLICED ZUCCHINI**
4 **TABLESPOONS OLIVE OIL**
4 **CLOVES GARLIC, MINCED**
4 **CHICKEN LEGS AND THIGHS**
SALT AND PEPPER TO TASTE
1 **MEDIUM TOMATO, PEELED AND SLICED**
2 **CUPS DRY WHITE WINE OR VERMOUTH**
¼ **TEASPOON DRIED BASIL**
¼ **TEASPOON DRIED ROSEMARY**
¼ **TEASPOON DRIED TARRAGON**
½ **CUP CHICKEN BROTH OR BOUILLON**

Slice zucchini ¼ inch thick. Pour half of the olive oil into a large skillet or Dutch oven. Sauté garlic and zucchini 8-10 minutes. Remove from pan.

Add additional olive oil and chicken pieces. Brown pieces thoroughly. Season with salt and pepper.

Layer zucchini and tomato slices over chicken, adding wine and other seasonings. Continue cooking over low heat 25-30 minutes until chicken is tender.

Transfer chicken and vegetables to serving platter. Add broth to the skillet and simmer, stirring frequently until sauce is smooth and somewhat reduced. Pour over zucchini and chicken. This may be served over rice, spaghetti, or noodles.

PREPARATION TIME: 30 MINUTES
COOKING TIME: 35-40 MINUTES
SERVES: 4

ZUCCHINI-GROUND VEAL ITALIAN

1   POUND GROUND VEAL
1½ CUPS TOMATO SAUCE
¼   CUP RED WINE
4   MEDIUM ZUCCHINI, THINLY
      SLICED
1   TEASPOON DRIED OREGANO
½   TEASPOON DRIED BASIL
1   TEASPOON GARLIC SALT
1¾ CUPS SHREDDED LOW-FAT
      MOZZARELLA CHEESE
¼   CUP GRATED PARMESAN
      CHEESE
¼   CUP SEASONED BREAD CRUMBS

Preheat oven to 350°F. Brown veal in a large skillet. In a large saucepan, combine tomato sauce, wine, zucchini, oregano, basil, and garlic salt. Simmer about 10 minutes. Add to veal.

Layer veal mixture and mozzarella in a well-greased 1½-quart casserole. Sprinkle with Parmesan cheese and bread crumbs. Bake in the oven for 20 minutes, or until cheese is melted. *Note:* A bottom layer of spaghetti squash would add interest and volume.

PREPARATION TIME: 20 MINUTES
BAKING TIME: 20 MINUTES
SERVES: 4

ZUCCHINI-SHRIMP SUPREME

6   CUPS ZUCCHINI, SLICED ½ INCH
      THICK OR
    2 CUPS MASHED COOKED
      WINTER SQUASH
½   CUP CHOPPED ONIONS
½   CUP CHOPPED GREEN PEPPERS
6   TABLESPOONS MELTED
      MARGARINE
1   CUP SOUR CREAM
1   CAN CONDENSED CREAM OF
      SHRIMP SOUP, UNDILUTED
2   CUPS SEASONED BREAD
      CRUMBS

Preheat oven to 350°F. In a large skillet, sauté zucchini, onions, and green peppers in 4 tablespoons margarine until tender.

Combine with sour cream, shrimp soup, and 1½ cups bread crumbs. Turn into a well-greased 1½-quart casserole. Top with remaining crumbs and margarine. Bake for 30 minutes.

PREPARATION TIME: 15 MINUTES
BAKING TIME: 30 MINUTES
SERVES: 6

SUMMER SQUASH STUFFED WITH GROUND MEAT

4   MEDIUM SUMMER SQUASH
    WATER
1   LARGE ONION, CHOPPED
1   CLOVE GARLIC, DICED
4   TOMATOES, PEELED AND
    CHOPPED
½   CUP CHOPPED GREEN PEPPERS
1   TABLESPOON VEGETABLE OIL
4-6 OUNCES COOKED MEAT,
    GROUND OR CHOPPED OR
    3 SLICES BACON, FRIED CRISP
    AND CRUMBLED
    SALT AND PEPPER TO TASTE
4   OUNCES DRY BREAD CRUMBS
4   OUNCES PARMESAN OR
    CHEDDAR CHEESE, GRATED

Preheat oven to 375°F. Simmer squash in boiling salted water about 12 minutes. Cut lengthwise. Scoop out pulp and chop.

In a large mixing bowl, combine pulp, onion, garlic, tomatoes, green peppers, oil, meat, and seasonings. Pile mixture into squash halves and place on a baking sheet. Top with bread crumbs and grated cheese. Bake approximately 15 minutes. *Note:* The proportions in this basic stuffing recipe may be altered to fit the size of the zucchini or the amount of ingredients you have on hand.

> *PREPARATION TIME: 20 MINUTES*
> *BAKING TIME: 15 MINUTES*
> *SERVES: 8*

ZUCCHINI LASAGNA

½   POUND GROUND BEEF
1   CUP TOMATO SAUCE
1   TEASPOON ITALIAN SEASONING
1   TEASPOON SALT
⅛   TEASPOON GARLIC POWDER
7-8 CUPS ZUCCHINI, SLICED
    LENGTHWISE
1   CUP SMALL CURD COTTAGE
    CHEESE
¾   CUP GRATED LOW-FAT
    MOZZARELLA CHEESE

Preheat oven to 325°F. Lightly brown ground beef in a medium skillet. Stir in tomato sauce and seasonings.

Arrange slices of zucchini in the bottom of an 8-inch baking dish. Spoon on half of beef mixture and half of cottage cheese. Sprinkle with half of mozzarella cheese. Repeat layering. Bake for 40 minutes.

> *PREPARATION TIME: 15 MINUTES*
> *BAKING TIME: 40 MINUTES*
> *SERVES: 4*

ZUCCHINI-LEFTOVER LAMB SCALLOP

1 CUP DRY BREAD CRUMBS
  COLD ROAST LAMB, SLICED OR
    CUBED (ABOUT ½ POUND)
3 MEDIUM ZUCCHINI, SLICED
2 MEDIUM TOMATOES, PEELED
    AND SLICED
1 TEASPOON ROSEMARY
  SALT AND PEPPER TO TASTE
  MARGARINE

Preheat oven to 350°F. Layer bread crumbs in the bottom of a baking pan or a well-greased 1-quart casserole. Alternate layers of meat, squash, and tomatoes.

Sprinkle meat layers with crushed rosemary leaves. Season vegetable layers with salt, pepper, and pats of margarine. Bake for 45 minutes.

> PREPARATION TIME: 10 MINUTES
> BAKING TIME: 45 MINUTES
> SERVES: 2

FISH STUFFED SQUASH

2 CUPS WATER
¾ CUP WHITE VINEGAR
3 TABLESPOONS SUGAR
1 BAY LEAF
1 CELERY STALK WITH LEAVES
¼ TEASPOON GROUND CORIANDER
¼ TEASPOON SALT
  PEPPER TO TASTE
2 MEDIUM SUMMER SQUASH
1½ CUPS FLAKED COOKED FISH
    (COD, HALIBUT, TURBOT, ETC.)
1 SMALL ONION, MINCED
2 TEASPOONS LEMON JUICE
½ CUP SOUR CREAM
¼ TEASPOON DRIED BASIL
  LETTUCE (OPTIONAL)
  TOMATO WEDGES (OPTIONAL)

Combine in a small saucepan, water, vinegar, sugar, bay leaf, celery, coriander, salt, and pepper. Bring to a rolling boil. Reduce heat and simmer for 8 minutes.

Slice squash lengthwise. In a large saucepan, place squash and cover with prepared liquid and simmer until almost tender. Scoop out pulp. Turn shells upside down to drain.

Combine pulp, fish, onion, lemon juice, and sour cream. Season. Fill squash with mixture. Chill thoroughly. Serve on fresh, crisp lettuce leaves with tomato wedges as garnish, if desired.

> PREPARATION TIME: 10 MINUTES
> COOKING TIME: 8 MINUTES
> MAKES: 4

THE PUMPKIN IS THE CASSEROLE

1   5-6 POUND PUMPKIN
    SALT AND PEPPER TO TASTE
    WATER
1   MEDIUM ONION, MINCED
1   GREEN PEPPER, MINCED
1   CLOVE GARLIC, MINCED
¼   CUP MARGARINE
1   POUND GROUND BEEF
½   TEASPOON GROUND THYME
½   TEASPOON SALT
¼   TEASPOON FRESHLY GROUND
       BLACK PEPPER
3   TOMATOES, PEELED AND
       QUARTERED
1   CUP BEEF BROTH OR BOUILLON
2   TABLESPOONS DRY WHITE WINE
1½ CUPS COOKED RICE
½   CUP GRATED CHEDDAR CHEESE

Preheat oven to 350°F. Remove lid of pumpkin and retain. Scoop out seeds and stringy portion. Score inside several times and rub interior with salt and pepper. Place pumpkin upside down in a large shallow pan with ¼-inch water. Place lid of pumpkin in pan beside pumpkin. Bake for 1 hour, or until tender. Drain.

In a large skillet, sauté onion, green pepper, and garlic in margarine. Add ground beef and seasonings and simmer until meat is lightly browned. Cook with tomatoes, broth, and wine until liquid is reduced considerably.

Stir in cooked rice and mix thoroughly. Stuff pumpkin with this mixture. Top with grated cheese and return to the oven until cheese is melted. Replace pumpkin lid until serving time. Serve from the pumpkin. The pumpkin pulp may be scooped out and served also.

PREPARATION TIME: 20 MINUTES
BAKING TIME: 1 HOUR
SERVES: 6

CHAPTER 7
VEGETABLE DISHES

No other vegetable, not even the tomato, is as adaptable to so many types of preparation as are squashes. Whether served raw, fresh from the garden, or baked and napped with the most sophisticated sauce, summer squash, zucchini in particular, has no equal in versatility. Winter varieties, although they cannot be recommended in a raw state, are delicious baked, stuffed, mashed, and fried, and therefore, are no slouches either, when it comes to providing interesting and nutritious dishes. Even the squash blossom makes its contribution as you will learn from several of the following recipes.

Whether you are preparing an elegant multicourse dinner or a do-it-yourself cook-out, include some squash on the menu. From appetizer to dessert, there is a squash recipe to fill the bill.

BASIC BAKED ZUCCHINI

1 **MEDIUM ZUCCHINI, THINLY SLICED**
1 **MEDIUM TOMATO, PEELED AND CHOPPED, OR SLICED**
1 **MEDIUM ONION, THINLY SLICED SALT AND PEPPER TO TASTE MARGARINE**
½ **CUP DRY BREAD CRUMBS**

Preheat oven to 350°F. In a well-greased 1-quart baking dish, layer zucchini, tomatoes, and onions until used up. Sprinkle each zucchini layer with salt and pepper and dot with margarine. Sprinkle crumbs on top. Bake uncovered until vegetables are done, about 20 minutes.

PREPARATION TIME: 15 MINUTES
BAKING TIME: 20 MINUTES
SERVES: 2

BASIC ZUCCHINI PLUS HERBS

¼ **TEASPOON GARLIC SALT**
1 **TEASPOON ITALIAN SEASONING**
 OR **1 TEASPOON DRIED BASIL, OREGANO, SAVORY, OR ROSEMARY,**
 OR **A COMBINATION OF THESE HERBS EQUAL TO 1 TEASPOON**

See basic recipe above.
Sprinkle herbs on the zucchini layers.

BASIC ZUCCHINI PLUS CHEESE

6 **OUNCES MUENSTER, MOZZARELLA, CHEDDAR, GRUYÈRE, SWISS, AMERICAN, ROMANO, OR PARMESAN CHEESE**

See basic recipe above.
Add a layer of cheese to the basic recipe and another on top. Then sprinkle with bread crumbs.

ZUCCHINI-BARLEY BAKE

1 CUP BARLEY (OR BULGUR)
2 CUPS WATER WITH SALT
1 SMALL ONION, MINCED
1 CLOVE GARLIC, MINCED
½ CUP CHOPPED GREEN PEPPERS
½ CUP CHOPPED CELERY
1 MEDIUM TOMATO, PEELED AND
   CHOPPED
2 SMALL ZUCCHINI, CHOPPED
1 TABLESPOON OLIVE OIL
¼ TEASPOON ITALIAN SEASONING
¾ CUP GRATED CHEDDAR CHEESE

Preheat oven to 350°F. Add barley to boiling salted water in a small saucepan. Reduce heat and simmer for 45 minutes.

Meanwhile, in a large skillet, cook the vegetables in oil until tender. Combine with barley. Season and place in a well-greased 1-quart casserole. Top with the cheese and bake for 20 minutes.

PREPARATION TIME: 45 MINUTES
BAKING TIME: 20 MINUTES
SERVES: 2-3

ZUCCHINI-CORN COMBO

3 MEDIUM ZUCCHINI, SLICED ½
   INCH THICK
WATER
½ CUP DICED ONIONS
1 TABLESPOON MARGARINE
2 CUPS COOKED FRESH CORN
2 EGGS, BEATEN
1 CUP SHREDDED LOW-FAT
   MOZZARELLA CHEESE
½ TEASPOON SALT
PEPPER TO TASTE
½ CUP FINE BUTTERED BREAD
   CRUMBS

Preheat oven to 350°F. In a large saucepan, simmer zucchini in boiling salted water until tender. Drain and mash.

In a large skillet, sauté onions in margarine and combine zucchini, corn, eggs, cheese, and seasonings. Pour mixture in a well-greased 1½-quart baking dish and top with buttered crumbs. Bake for 35-40 minutes.

PREPARATION TIME: 20 MINUTES
BAKING TIME: 35-40 MINUTES
SERVES: 4

CHAYOTE OR SUMMER SQUASH BAKE

1 CUP BISCUIT MIX
½ CUP CHOPPED ONIONS
½ CUP GRATED PARMESAN
    CHEESE
2 TABLESPOONS MINCED FRESH
    PARSLEY
½ TEASPOON SEASONED SALT
½ TEASPOON DRIED OREGANO
    PEPPER TO TASTE
1 CLOVE GARLIC, MINCED
½ CUP VEGETABLE OIL
4 EGGS, BEATEN
3 CUPS SLICED SUMMER SQUASH

Preheat oven to 350°F. Mix ingredients in a large mixing bowl and pour into a buttered 13 x 9 x 2-inch baking dish. Bake for 25 minutes.

PREPARATION TIME: 10 MINUTES
BAKING TIME: 25 MINUTES
SERVES: 4

CHEESE AND SQUASH RELLENO

1½ CUPS COOKED RICE
1 7-OUNCE CAN MILD CHILIES,
    CHOPPED
6½ CUPS GRATED MONTEREY JACK
    CHEESE
3 MEDIUM SUMMER SQUASH,
    PARBOILED
1 MEDIUM TOMATO, SLICED
2 CUPS SOUR CREAM
⅓ CUP CHOPPED GREEN PEPPERS
2 TABLESPOONS CHOPPED
    ONIONS
1 TABLESPOON DRIED PARSLEY
1 TEASPOON DRIED OREGANO
1 TEASPOON SALT

Preheat oven to 350°F. Spread cooked rice in bottom of a buttered baking dish. Layer chilies, 5½ cups of cheese, the squash, and the tomato on top of the rice.

Combine sour cream, green peppers, onions, parsley, oregano, and salt. Spoon over squash mixture. Sprinkle with remaining 1 cup of cheese. Bake for 30 minutes.

PREPARATION TIME: 15 MINUTES
BAKING TIME: 30 MINUTES
SERVES: 6

ZUCCHINI BASIL TART

**SALT FOR SPRINKLING ON
TOMATOES AND ZUCCHINI**

1 **MEDIUM ZUCCHINI, THINLY
SLICED**

1 **POUND TOMATOES, SLICED**

1 **CUP FIRMLY PACKED FRESH
BASIL (EXTRA SPRIGS FOR
GARNISH)**

½ **CUP, PLUS 2 TABLESPOONS
PART-SKIM MILK RICOTTA
CHEESE**

2 **LARGE EGGS**

¼ **POUND PART-SKIM MILK
MOZZARELLA CHEESE,
COARSELY GRATED**

½ **CUP GRATED PARMESAN
CHEESE**

1 **UNBAKED 9-INCH PIE SHELL
OIL FOR BRUSHING TOMATOES**

Preheat oven to 350°F. Drain salted zucchini and tomato slices on paper towels.

Puree basil in a food processor with ricotta and eggs. Add mozzarella and Parmesan cheese. Blend until just combined.

Line a 9-inch pie shell with zucchini slices. Spoon basil mixture over zucchini. Arrange tomato slices on top. Brush with oil. Bake 40-50 minutes. Let stand 15 minutes. Garnish with basil.

PREPARATION TIME: 30 MINUTES
BAKING TIME: 40-50 MINUTES
SERVES: 6

SURPRISE SQUASH PIE

2 DOZEN TRISCUIT CRACKERS, CRUSHED
3 TABLESPOONS MELTED SWEET BUTTER
1 CUP CHOPPED RED ONIONS
3 TABLESPOONS OLIVE OIL
2 CUPS CHOPPED RED BELL PEPPERS
2 MEDIUM ZUCCHINI, CHOPPED
2 TEASPOONS MINCED GARLIC
SALT AND PEPPER TO TASTE
2 TABLESPOONS GRATED PARMESAN CHEESE
3 TABLESPOONS CHOPPED FRESH BASIL

Preheat oven to 350°F. In a small mixing bowl, stir cracker crumbs and butter together and press mixture into a 9-inch pie pan and bake shell 10 minutes.

In a large skillet, sauté onions in oil, add peppers, and continue cooking for several minutes. Add zucchini and cook an additional 5 minutes. Add garlic, plus salt and pepper, and continue cooking for several more minutes.

Stir in cheese and basil and spoon filling into the pie shell. Bake for 5 minutes.

PREPARATION TIME: 25 MINUTES
BAKING TIME: 15 MINUTES
SERVES: 2

SWEET POTATO SQUASH BAKE

2 CUPS COOKED, PEELED, AND MASHED DELICATA (SWEET POTATO SQUASH)
3 TABLESPOONS MELTED MARGARINE
2 TABLESPOONS BROWN SUGAR
½ TEASPOON SALT
⅛ TEASPOON FRESHLY GROUND BLACK PEPPER
¼ TEASPOON GROUND NUTMEG
1 EGG, BEATEN
½ CUP CHOPPED NUTS
1 CUP DRAINED CRUSHED PINEAPPLE

Preheat oven to 350°F. In a medium mixing bowl, combine mashed squash pulp with remaining ingredients. Pour into a well-greased baking dish. Bake for 30 minutes.

PREPARATION TIME: 20 MINUTES
BAKING TIME: 30 MINUTES
SERVES: 4

ZUCCHINI TART NIÇOISE

1   CLOVE GARLIC, MINCED
2   MEDIUM ONIONS, MINCED
2½ TABLESPOONS OLIVE OIL
2   MEDIUM GREEN PEPPERS,
      SLICED
1   SMALL EGGPLANT, PEELED AND
      DICED
2   MEDIUM ZUCCHINI, SLICED
1   CUP PEELED AND SEEDED
      TOMATOES OR EQUIVALENT
      TOMATO SAUCE
      SALT AND PEPPER TO TASTE
1   BAKED 9-INCH PIE SHELL
      PARMESAN CHEESE, GRATED
      OLIVE OIL

In a large skillet, sauté garlic and onions in olive oil. Add the next five ingredients and simmer until liquid is almost evaporated and vegetables are tender, about 45 minutes.

Spoon into baked pie shell and bake in moderate oven 10 minutes. Top with cheese and a little olive oil. Bake for 5 minutes more.

PREPARATION TIME: 15 MINUTES
COOKING TIME: 45 MINUTES
BAKING TIME: 15 MINUTES
SERVES: 6

ZUCCHINI CHEESE SQUARES

1   CUP COARSELY GRATED AND
      DRAINED ZUCCHINI
1   CUP GRATED CARROTS
3   EGGS
1   CUP CHOPPED ONIONS
⅓ CUP DRIED DILL WEED
½ CUP CHOPPED MINT LEAVES
½ CUP CHOPPED FRESH PARSLEY
1   CUP GRATED MUENSTER
      CHEESE
½ CUP MASHED FETA CHEESE
      SALT, PEPPER, AND PAPRIKA TO
      TASTE
1½ CUPS ALL-PURPOSE FLOUR

Preheat oven to 350°F. Place all ingredients in a large mixing bowl, mixing well with flour. Turn into a well-greased 9-inch square baking dish. Bake for 50 minutes, or until browned. Cut into squares.

PREPARATION TIME: 20 MINUTES
BAKING TIME: 50 MINUTES
SERVES: 6

RATATOUILLE

1 **MEDIUM ZUCCHINI, DICED**
1 **MEDIUM EGGPLANT, PEELED AND DICED**
2 **TABLESPOONS OLIVE OIL**
1 **6-OUNCE CAN TOMATO PASTE**
¼ **CUP CHOPPED ONIONS**
¼ **CUP CHOPPED GREEN PEPPERS**
1 **CLOVE GARLIC, MINCED**
1 **TEASPOON SALT**
½ **TEASPOON FRESHLY GROUND BLACK PEPPER**
½ **CUP DRY RED WINE**
½ **CUP SOUR CREAM**
1 **8-OUNCE CAN TOMATO SAUCE**
1 **CUP SHREDDED LOW-FAT MOZZARELLA CHEESE**

Preheat oven to 350°F. In a large skillet, sauté zucchini and eggplant in oil. Stir in the next eight ingredients and heat thoroughly.

Turn into a well-greased 1½-quart baking dish and top with tomato sauce and cheese. Bake 45 minutes.

> *PREPARATION TIME: 20 MINUTES*
> *BAKING TIME: 45 MINUTES*
> *SERVES: 2*

SQUASH ORIENTAL

2 **MEDIUM ACORN SQUASH OR SMALL PUMPKINS, CUT IN HALF LENGTHWISE**
1½ **TABLESPOONS MELTED MARGARINE**
1½ **TABLESPOONS LIGHT BROWN SUGAR**
1 **TABLESPOON SHERRY**
¼ **TEASPOON GROUND GINGER**
SALT AND PEPPER TO TASTE

Preheat oven to 375°F. Bake squash halves 30 minutes.

In a small mixing bowl, combine other ingredients. Fill squash halves with margarine mixture and bake for 25 minutes, or until squash is done.

> *PREPARATION TIME: 10 MINUTES*
> *BAKING TIME: 55 MINUTES TOTAL*
> *SERVES: 4*

GREEK BAKED ZUCCHINI

4 LARGE TOMATOES, PEELED AND
    CHOPPED
1 CLOVE GARLIC, MINCED
½ CUP OLIVE OIL
1 TEASPOON SUGAR
½ TEASPOON DRIED OREGANO
½ TEASPOON DRIED MINT
    SALT AND PEPPER TO TASTE
6 CUPS ZUCCHINI, SLICED ¼ INCH
    THICK
2 MEDIUM ONIONS, SLICED
4 OUNCES FETA CHEESE,
    CRUMBLED
½ CUP DRY BREAD CRUMBS
1 TABLESPOON MARGARINE

Preheat oven to 350°F. Combine first seven ingredients in a large mixing bowl. Grease a 9 x 13 x 2-inch baking dish and layer zucchini, tomato mixture, and sliced onions.

Crumble feta cheese on top, sprinkle with bread crumbs, and dot with dabs of margarine. Bake for 45 minutes, or until squash is tender.

PREPARATION TIME: 20 MINUTES
BAKING TIME: 45 MINUTES
SERVES: 6

BUTTERNUT AND SWEET POTATOES MASHED

1 CUP COOKED AND MASHED
    BUTTERNUT SQUASH
1 CUP COOKED AND MASHED
    SWEET POTATOES
¼ CUP SOFTENED MARGARINE
½ TEASPOON SALT
¼ TEASPOON GROUND NUTMEG
¼ TEASPOON GROUND CINNAMON
⅛ TEASPOON FRESHLY GROUND
    BLACK PEPPER

In a large mixing bowl, whip all ingredients together until fluffy. Heat mixture in a double boiler. For flavor variations, try mint, cloves, ginger, poppy, or sesame seed, bits of orange or lemon peel, or grated apple.

PREPARATION TIME: 30 MINUTES
COOKING TIME: 15 MINUTES
SERVES: 4

CITRUS SQUASH BAKE

3 MEDIUM ACORN SQUASH
  WATER
6 TABLESPOONS BUTTER OR
  MARGARINE
6 TABLESPOONS BROWN SUGAR
1 TABLESPOON GRATED ORANGE
  PEEL
½ TEASPOON SALT
3 ORANGES, PEELED AND
  SECTIONED
1 GRAPEFRUIT, PEELED AND
  SECTIONED
¼ CUP GOLDEN RAISINS

Preheat oven to 375°F. Place whole squash in a large baking pan. Add ¼-inch water. Bake 45 minutes.

Remove squash from oven and cut each in half horizontally. Scoop out seeds and discard. Return squash halves to baking pan with cut side up. Fill each cavity with 1 tablespoon brown sugar, 1 tablespoon butter or margarine, and divide orange peel equally. Sprinkle cavities with salt. Divide sectioned fruit equally and bake squash for an additional 25 minutes.

PREPARATION TIME: 20 MINUTES
BAKING TIME: 1 HOUR 10 MINUTES TOTAL
SERVES: 6

SWEET BAKED ACORN SQUASH

1 MEDIUM ACORN SQUASH, CUT IN
  HALF LENGTHWISE
1 TABLESPOON MELTED
  MARGARINE
¼ CUP MILK
¼ CUP MAPLE SYRUP

Preheat oven to 350°F. Scoop out seeds and stringy portion of squash. Place cut side down on a baking sheet. Bake 45 minutes. Turn squash. Fill with remaining ingredients and bake another 15 minutes. *Note:* Other sweeteners for this popular recipe are brown sugar, currant jelly, crushed pineapple, mint jelly, applesauce, apple butter, or chutney. Omit the milk with these sweeteners.

PREPARATION TIME: 10 MINUTES
BAKING TIME: 1 HOUR TOTAL
SERVES: 2

TOASTED ALMOND SQUASH

1 MEDIUM BUTTERNUT SQUASH,
   CUT IN HALF LENGTHWISE
   WATER
3 TABLESPOONS MARGARINE
½ CUP MAPLE SYRUP
   DASH GROUND NUTMEG
⅓ CUP TOASTED ALMONDS

Preheat oven to 350°F. In a large saucepan, cook squash in boiling salted water until tender. Scoop out pulp and beat pulp with margarine until smooth. Stir in syrup and nutmeg.

Fill squash halves with this mixture and top with slivered toasted almonds. Bake until heated through. *Note:* A well-greased 1-quart casserole may be substituted for the squash shells if more convenient.

```
PREPARATION TIME: 25 MINUTES
COOKING TIME: 20 MINUTES
SERVES: 2
```

BAKED SQUASH AND ONIONS AU GRATIN

   WINTER SQUASH OR PUMPKIN
   WEDGES TO SERVE 4
10 SMALL OR 5 MEDIUM ONIONS,
   STEAMED
1 TABLESPOON MARGARINE
1 TABLESPOON ALL-PURPOSE
   FLOUR
¾ CUP MILK
½ CUP GRATED MILD CHEDDAR
   CHEESE
   SALT, PEPPER, AND PAPRIKA TO
   TASTE

Preheat oven to 350°F. Bake squash or pumpkin wedges about 40 minutes. Steam onions on a rack over boiling water 30 minutes.

Melt margarine. Mix with flour and gradually add milk. Blend in cheese and seasonings, stirring continually. Spoon hot sauce and onions over squash wedges.

```
PREPARATION TIME: 10 MINUTES
COOKING TIME: 30 MINUTES
BAKING TIME: 40 MINUTES
SERVES: 4
```

ZUCCHINI AND ARTICHOKES

1 9-OUNCE PACKAGE FROZEN
   ARTICHOKE HEARTS
2 TABLESPOONS WATER
4 CUPS SLICED ZUCCHINI
2 CUPS FRESH OR CANNED
   MUSHROOMS
2 TABLESPOONS MINCED ONIONS
1 CLOVE GARLIC, MINCED
   SALT AND PEPPER TO TASTE
   OLIVE OIL
2 MEDIUM TOMATOES, WEDGED
   AND SEEDED
⅓ CUP GRATED PARMESAN
   CHEESE

In a large saucepan, cook artichokes according to directions on package. Add zucchini, mushrooms, and onions. Cook until tender.

Drain and add garlic. Season. Drizzle with olive oil. Add tomatoes and sprinkle with cheese.

PREPARATION TIME: 25 MINUTES
COOKING TIME: 15 MINUTES
SERVES: 6

CANDIED PUMPKIN

1 SMALL PUMPKIN OR MEDIUM
   WINTER SQUASH
⅓ CUP PACKED BROWN SUGAR
¼ CUP CHOPPED PRESERVED
   GINGER
¾ CUP MELTED MARGARINE

Preheat oven to 350°F. Cut pumpkin or squash into wedges large enough for an individual serving. Lightly grease a large baking dish and place pumpkin in, skin side down.

In a small saucepan, stir brown sugar and ginger in margarine over low heat until sugar is dissolved. Ladle over wedges and bake, covered, until tender, approximately 1 hour.

PREPARATION TIME: 10 MINUTES
BAKING TIME: 1 HOUR
SERVES: 4

SUMMER SQUASH IN WINE-MUSTARD SAUCE

1 CUP GREEN BEANS
½ CUP WATER
3 MEDIUM ZUCCHINI, CUT INTO ¼-INCH SLICES
1 MEDIUM YELLOW SUMMER SQUASH, CUT INTO ¼-INCH SLICES
1 SMALL ONION, CHOPPED

SAUCE:

½ CUP CHICKEN BROTH
3 TABLESPOONS DRY WHITE WINE
1 SMALL ONION, CHOPPED
1½ TABLESPOONS CORNSTARCH
½ TEASPOON DRIED TARRAGON
2 TEASPOONS DIJON MUSTARD
¼ TEASPOON FRESHLY GROUND BLACK PEPPER
1 TABLESPOON MARGARINE

Place beans and water in a 2-quart microwave casserole. In a microwave oven, cook, covered, on HIGH for 8 minutes. Add zucchini, squash, and onion and cook 5-7 minutes more. Drain.

Sauce:

Combine first seven ingredients in a 2-cup glass measure. In a microwave oven, cook, uncovered, for 2-3 minutes until thick and bubbly, stirring every minute. Stir in margarine. Toss with vegetables.

PREPARATION TIME: 15 MINUTES
COOKING TIME: 18 MINUTES
SERVES: 6 SIDE DISHES

BAKED PUMPKIN

1 PUMPKIN, CUT INTO WEDGES
HONEY
NUTMEG
RAISINS
SALT

Preheat oven to 350°F. On a baking sheet, bake wedges until pulp is soft, about 20 minutes. Remove skin from pulp. Mash with remaining ingredients according to preferences of flavors and consistency. Serve on toast or English muffins.

PREPARATION TIME: 10 MINUTES
BAKING TIME: 20 MINUTES
SERVES: VARIABLE

SQUASH BLOSSOMS

Squash plants bear male and female blossoms. The stem of the female flower eventually begins to swell. This swelling is the squash forming in its initial growth stage. The dried female flower often must be plucked from the end of the mature vegetable. Male blossoms, having long since met their responsibilities in the pollination process, simply fall off and decay. Many gardeners are distressed by this event on the erroneous assumption that these fallen blossoms represent squash which failed to mature.

When first blooming, squash may produce only male blossoms. These may all fall off. The gardener should not be disappointed as this is a common occurrence. Have faith that the female blossoms will appear. Since it is the female blossom which produces squash, pick only surplus male blossoms for cooking purposes. Be sure to leave at least one of these to a plant for fertilization purposes.

The male blossoms, easily identified by long, slender stems, can be used by the cook to make several dishes for the table. They may be dipped in thin batter and fried, or picked while still in the budding stage and sautéed. Stuffing possibilities are limited only by one's imagination.

A new hybrid, Butter-blossom zucchini, has been developed specifically for abundant blossoms. Actually all squash produce edible blossoms.

In addition to the following recipes, blossoms also may be sliced into strips and used in omelettes, pastas, and soups.

See chapter 10 for squash blossom soup recipes.

These delicate blossoms lend themselves very well to a meat stuffing and, as such, may be served as a main dish. Leftover ham, lamb, or chicken can be used to make a delicious forcemeat.

SQUASH BLOSSOMS WITH ITALIAN SAUSAGE

3 PARTS GROUND ITALIAN
   SAUSAGE
1 PART CHOPPED ONIONS
1 PART CHOPPED GREEN PEPPERS
   TOMATO SAUCE
   PARMESAN CHEESE, GRATED
   SQUASH BLOSSOMS

Preheat oven to 325°F. Prepare amounts needed using these proportions. Crumble sausage in a large skillet and sauté until lightly browned with onions and green peppers. Drain off excess fat.

Add enough tomato sauce to bind mixture. Season with cheese. Stuff blossoms. Place in a well-greased baking dish and bake 10 minutes, or until heated through.

> PREPARATION TIME: 30 MINUTES
> BAKING TIME: 10 MINUTES
> SERVES: VARIABLE

BLOSSOMS AND CREAM CHEESE

1 8-OUNCE PACKAGE CREAM
   CHEESE, SOFTENED
⅓ CUP MINCED ONIONS
   SALT AND PEPPER TO TASTE
   CHIVES TO TASTE
   CAPERS (OPTIONAL)
12-14 SQUASH BLOSSOMS

Preheat oven to 300°F. Mix cream cheese, onions, seasonings, and chives. Stuff squash blossoms. Sauté gently or place in a well-greased baking dish. Bake 10 minutes, or until heated through.

> PREPARATION TIME: 15 MINUTES
> BAKING TIME: 10 MINUTES
> SERVES: 6-7

TUNA STUFFED BLOSSOMS

1 7-OUNCE CAN TUNA, WATER-
    PACKED
1 TEASPOON GRATED
    HORSERADISH
½ CUP LOW-FAT PLAIN YOGURT
½ CUP LOW-CALORIE MAYONNAISE
½ CUP DICED CELERY
¼ CUP MINCED ONIONS
¼ CUP OLIVE OIL
12 SQUASH BLOSSOMS

Preheat oven to 325°F. In a medium mixing bowl, combine first four ingredients and set aside.

In a small skillet, briefly sauté the celery and onions in oil. Add this combination to tuna mixture.

Stuff blossoms and place in a well-greased baking dish. Bake 10 minutes, or until heated through.

PREPARATION TIME: 15 MINUTES

BAKING TIME: 10 MINUTES

SERVES: 6

BLOSSOMS WITH SPINACH AND RICE

1 TABLESPOON CHOPPED ONIONS
1½ TABLESPOONS MARGARINE
2 CUPS COOKED, CHOPPED, AND
    DRAINED SPINACH OR SWISS
    CHARD
1 CUP COOKED RICE
1 EGG YOLK
½ CUP GRATED GRUYERE CHEESE
    SALT AND PEPPER TO TASTE
8-12 SQUASH BLOSSOMS

Preheat oven to 325°F. In a large skillet, sauté onions in margarine. Add spinach and rice. Mix well. Stir in egg yolk, cheese, salt, and pepper.

Stuff blossoms and place in a well-greased baking dish. Bake 10 minutes, or until heated through.

PREPARATION TIME: 20 MINUTES

BAKING TIME: 10 MINUTES

SERVES: 4-6

ZUCCHINI CHARCOAL-GRILLED

ZUCCHINI, CROOKNECK, OR
   OTHER SUMMER SQUASH,
   SLICED
TOMATOES, QUARTERED
GREEN PEPPERS, QUARTERED
SMALL ONIONS
NEW POTATOES
SALT AND PEPPER

Wrap each vegetable in buttered heavy-duty aluminum foil. Place foil package on coals to bake. Potatoes need about 40 minutes, rest of vegetables 20 minutes. They can be baked together by starting the potatoes first. Turn package once during baking.

> *PREPARATION TIME: 10 MINUTES*
> *COOKING TIME: 40 MINUTES TOTAL*
> *SERVES: VARIABLE*

ZUCCHINI SHASHLIK

1 MEDIUM GREEN ZUCCHINI, CUT
   INTO CHUNKS
1 MEDIUM GOLDEN ZUCCHINI OR
   OTHER YELLOW SUMMER
   SQUASH, CUT INTO CHUNKS
8 CHERRY TOMATOES
1 MEDIUM GREEN PEPPER, CUT
   INTO SMALL SQUARES
4 MEDIUM ONIONS, QUARTERED
1 CUP ITALIAN SALAD DRESSING

Marinate vegetables in Italian or other oil-vinegar dressing for at least an hour. Arrange vegetables on skewers. Grill over charcoal about 20 minutes.

> *PREPARATION TIME: 1 HOUR 10 MINUTES*
> *COOKING TIME: 20 MINUTES*
> *SERVES: 4*

BUTTERNUT SQUASH KEBOBS

BUTTERNUT SQUASH
SMALL TURNIPS
SWEET POTATOES
APPLES
BUTTER, MELTED

Scrub vegetables and apples. Do not peel.

Cut squash in half. Remove seeds and stringy portion. Cut into chunks. Leave turnips whole. Combine on skewers.

Halve or quarter sweet potatoes. Quarter and core apples. Alternate on skewers.

Grill over charcoal, apples and sweet potatoes, brushed with butter, 30-40 minutes; squash and turnips 25 minutes. If preferred, vegetables and apples may be combined in aluminum foil packages to which pats of butter have been added.

PREPARATION TIME: 10 MINUTES
COOKING TIME: 40 MINUTES
SERVES: VARIABLE

FRENCH-FRIED ZUCCHINI

2 CUPS ZUCCHINI OR OTHER SUMMER SQUASH, CUT INTO ½-INCH SLICES
1 CUP ALL-PURPOSE FLOUR
¾ TEASPOON SALT
⅛ TEASPOON FRESHLY GROUND BLACK PEPPER
2 EGG YOLKS, BEATEN
6 OUNCES BEER
2 TABLESPOONS MELTED MARGARINE
2 EGG WHITES, STIFFLY BEATEN

Dry zucchini slices on paper towels. In a medium mixing bowl, combine flour, salt, pepper, egg yolks, and beer. Stir thoroughly. Add melted margarine and let mixture rest 1 hour at room temperature.

Fold in egg whites. Dip squash slices into batter and deep fry at 360°F. until browned, about 5 minutes.

PREPARATION TIME: 1 HOUR 15 MINUTES
COOKING TIME: 5 MINUTES
SERVES: 2

FRIED ZUCCHINI PARMESAN

1 MEDIUM ZUCCHINI, SLICED ½
  INCH THICK
1 CLOVE GARLIC, MINCED
3 TABLESPOONS HOT VEGETABLE
  OIL
  SALT AND PEPPER TO TASTE
1 TABLESPOON CHOPPED FRESH
  PARSLEY
1 TABLESPOON GRATED
  PARMESAN CHEESE

In a medium skillet, fry zucchini and garlic in hot oil until slightly brown. Season and serve sprinkled with parsley and Parmesan.

PREPARATION TIME: 10 MINUTES
COOKING TIME: 5 MINUTES
SERVES: 2

SQUASH FRITTERS

1 WINTER SQUASH OR 2 MEDIUM
  SUMMER SQUASHES, COOKED
  AND MASHED
1 EGG, BEATEN
1 TABLESPOON MINCED ONIONS
2 TABLESPOONS MILK
½ CUP ALL-PURPOSE FLOUR
  SALT AND PEPPER TO TASTE
1 TEASPOON BAKING POWDER
  VEGETABLE OIL

In a medium mixing bowl, mix squash, egg, onions, milk, flour, salt, pepper, and baking powder until well blended.

Drop batter by the spoonful into hot oil and fry 3-5 minutes, or until golden brown. Turn each fritter once. Drain on paper towels.

PREPARATION TIME: 20 MINUTES
COOKING TIME: 10 MINUTES
SERVES: 4

ZUCCHINI FRITTERS

½ CUP ALL-PURPOSE FLOUR
½ TEASPOON SALT
¼ TEASPOON GARLIC POWDER
1 CLOVE GARLIC, MINCED
  WATER
1 EGG
⅛ TEASPOON FRESHLY GROUND
  BLACK PEPPER
½ TEASPOON DRIED OREGANO
¼ TEASPOON GRATED PARMESAN
  CHEESE
1 MEDIUM ZUCCHINI, THINLY
  SLICED
  VEGETABLE OIL

In a medium mixing bowl, combine all ingredients except sliced squash and oil.

Heat oil in a skillet, dip squash in batter and fry until golden brown. Turn each fritter once. Drain on paper towels.

PREPARATION TIME: 15 MINUTES
COOKING TIME: 10 MINUTES
SERVES: 2

ZUCCHINI-VEGETABLE MIXES FOR FREEZING

Many delicious dishes can be prepared easily and quickly from frozen vegetable combinations. These may be served as entities in themselves or combined with meat and other ingredients to become mouthwatering sauces, stews, soups, and casseroles.

When the copious bounty of the squash patch becomes threatening, make several batches of one or more zucchini-vegetable mixes and stack them away in the freezer. Make a list of what you are storing and where, perhaps taping this list to the freezer itself so that anytime you need a vegetable mix, it can be located easily, already partially cooked, and ready to pop into a pot or baking dish at a moment's notice.

BASIC ZUCCHINI-VEGETABLE MIX

1 CUP MINCED ONIONS
1 CUP DICED CELERY
2 TABLESPOONS MELTED MARGARINE
2 CUPS CHICKEN BROTH OR BOUILLON
2 CUPS SLICED OR DICED CARROTS
2 CUPS ZUCCHINI OR OTHER SUMMER SQUASH, SLICED OR DICED
1 CUP CORN, CUT FROM COB
1 CUP CHOPPED GREEN PEPPERS SALT AND PEPPER TO TASTE

In a large skillet, sauté onions and celery in margarine. Add broth and carrots. Simmer for 20 minutes.

Add zucchini, corn, and green peppers and simmer an additional 10 minutes.

Season. Pour into freezer containers for future use in stews, soups, casseroles, or squash fillings. *Note:* Creamed mixed vegetables are delicious in squash halves.

PREPARATION TIME: 20 MINUTES
COOKING TIME: 30 MINUTES

ZUCCHINI-LEGUME MIX

1 CUP MINCED ONIONS
1 CUP CHOPPED CELERY
2 TABLESPOONS OLIVE OIL
2 CUPS SLICED ZUCCHINI
2 CUPS CHICKEN BROTH OR
   BOUILLON
1 CUP PEAS
1 CUP LIMA BEANS
1 CUP SLICED CARROTS
SALT AND PEPPER TO TASTE

In a large skillet, sauté onions and celery in oil. Sauté zucchini in the oil briefly. Add broth and remaining vegetables. Simmer for 20 minutes.

Season. Cool and pour all ingredients in freezer containers.

PREPARATION TIME: 20 MINUTES
COOKING TIME: 20 MINUTES

ZUCCHINI MIX IN TOMATO SAUCE

3 POUNDS RIPE TOMATOES,
   PEELED AND CHOPPED
¼ CUP MINCED ONIONS
1 CUP CHOPPED CELERY
2 TABLESPOONS OLIVE OIL
5-6 CUPS CHOPPED ZUCCHINI
1 TABLESPOON SUGAR OR HONEY
1½ TEASPOONS SALT

Force chopped tomatoes through a food mill or coarse sieve to remove seeds.

In a large skillet, sauté onions and celery in oil. Add zucchini, the tomato puree, and sugar. Simmer until reduced and thick, stirring frequently.

Add salt. Remove from heat and cool. Ladle into hot sterilized jars or appropriate freezer container, leaving ¼-inch headroom for expansion.

PREPARATION TIME: 20 MINUTES
COOKING TIME: 30 MINUTES

SUMMER SQUASH-ORIENTAL MIX

2 CUPS SLICED OR DICED SUMMER
    SQUASH
2 CUPS SHREDDED CABBAGE
1 CUP CHOPPED FRESH SPINACH
2 CUPS CHICKEN BROTH OR
    BOUILLON
1 CAN BEAN SPROUTS
1 CAN WATER CHESTNUTS, SLICED
SALT AND PEPPER TO TASTE

In a large saucepan, simmer squash, cabbage, and spinach in broth until soft.

Add drained sprouts and chestnuts. Season. Freeze. May be heated and served alone or over rice.

PREPARATION TIME: 20 MINUTES
COOKING TIME: 10 MINUTES

SUMMER SQUASH-ITALIANO MIX

1 MEDIUM ONION, CHOPPED
2 CUPS SLICED OR DICED SUMMER
    SQUASH
2 TABLESPOONS OLIVE OIL
1 CUP COOKED GARBANZO BEANS
2 CUPS ROMANO GREEN BEANS,
    CUT INTO 2-INCH PIECES
1 MEDIUM RED BELL PEPPER,
    CHOPPED
2 CUPS CHICKEN BROTH OR
    BOUILLON
    SALT AND PEPPER TO TASTE
½ CUP SLICED OR CHOPPED
    GREEN OLIVES

In a large skillet, sauté onion and squash in oil until soft. Add more oil if necessary.

Add both beans, bell pepper, and broth. Simmer until vegetables are tender. Season.

Add olives. Pour into freezer containers and freeze.

PREPARATION TIME: 20 MINUTES
COOKING TIME: 10 MINUTES

PUREED SOUP BASE

3 LARGE ONIONS, THINLY SLICED
6 TABLESPOONS BUTTER OR
   VEGETABLE OIL
¼ CUP WATER
18 CUPS THINLY SLICED SUMMER
   SQUASH
2 MEDIUM GREEN PEPPERS,
   THINLY SLICED
3 CLOVES GARLIC, MINCED
2¼ TEASPOONS SALT
½ TEASPOON FRESHLY GROUND
   BLACK PEPPER
1 CUP MINCED FRESH HERBS
   (PARSLEY, BASIL, OR
   TARRAGON)

In a large skillet, sauté onions until soft in butter or vegetable oil. Add water, squash, peppers, garlic, salt, and pepper. Cover mixture and cook slowly for 3 minutes. Remove from heat and add fresh parsley, basil, or tarragon.

Puree mixture in processor, blender, or food mill. Cool mixture to room temperature and pack in pint freezer containers.

For soup. Combine 1½ cups of milk with each pint of puree. Add 1 cup of chicken broth or its equivalent in granules. Season to taste and serve soup hot.

For a baked squash dish. Add 2 beaten eggs to 1 pint of thawed puree. Pour mixture into a greased baking dish. Sprinkle with ½ cup Parmesan cheese. Place dish in a larger container with 1 inch of water and bake at 350°F. for 30 minutes.

> *PREPARATION TIME: 20 MINUTES*
> *COOKING TIME: 3 MINUTES*

BUTTERED BABY ZUCCHINI

8 SMALL ZUCCHINI
  WATER
1 MEDIUM ONION, CUT INTO
  RINGS
3 TABLESPOONS MELTED BUTTER
  GARLIC SALT TO TASTE

In a large saucepan, halve zucchini lengthwise and cook until tender in lightly salted water. Sauté onion rings in 1 tablespoon of butter in a small skillet. To serve, place squash on individual plates. Top with sautéed onion rings and nap with sauce of garlic salt and melted butter.

> *PREPARATION TIME: 10 MINUTES*
> *COOKING TIME: 5 MINUTES*
> *SERVES: 2*

ZUCCHINI MOUSSE

3 CUPS THINLY SLICED ZUCCHINI
8 CUPS WATER
2 TABLESPOONS SALT
½ STICK SWEET BUTTER, CHOPPED
   INTO PIECES
   CARROT STICKS, BLANCHED
   (OPTIONAL)
   GREEN ONIONS (OPTIONAL)

In a large saucepan, blanch zucchini for 3 minutes in boiling salted water. Drain and set aside for 20 minutes to drain thoroughly. Press out remaining moisture.

In a food processor or blender, puree squash and pour into a large steel or enamel saucepan. Bring to a boil and remove from heat.

Stir in butter pieces, one at a time. Serve mousse in custard cups or ramekins. Garnish with blanched carrot strips and fresh green onions.

PREPARATION TIME: 25 MINUTES
COOKING TIME: 10 MINUTES
SERVES: 4

ZUCCHINI SWEET AND SOUR

3 MEDIUM ZUCCHINI
¼ CUP VEGETABLE OIL
2 TABLESPOONS WHITE VINEGAR
2 TABLESPOONS SUGAR
   CHOPPED FRESH BASIL TO
   TASTE
   SALT AND PEPPER TO TASTE

Cut zucchini into ½-inch rounds or strips. In a medium skillet, sauté in oil until lightly brown and soft. Remove.

Add remaining ingredients to skillet and simmer 3 minutes. Season.

PREPARATION TIME: 5 MINUTES
COOKING TIME: 5 MINUTES
SERVES: 4

GREEN AND YELLOW SQUASH IN CREAM

1 **MEDIUM ZUCCHINI OR COCOZELLE, THINLY SLICED**
1 **MEDIUM YELLOW SUMMER SQUASH, THINLY SLICED (CROOKNECK, GOLDEN ZUCCHINI, OR STRAIGHTNECK)**
2 **TABLESPOONS MELTED MARGARINE**
¼ **TEASPOON SALT**
¼ **TEASPOON FRESHLY GROUND BLACK PEPPER**
1 **CUP CREAM**
½ **TEASPOON FRESH DILL OR ¼ TEASPOON DILL SEED**

Drain squash slices on paper towels. In a medium skillet, sauté in melted margarine. Season with salt and pepper.

Add cream and simmer mixture over low heat for 15 minutes. Mix well with dill. Serve hot.

> *PREPARATION TIME: 10 MINUTES*
> *COOKING TIME: 15 MINUTES*
> *SERVES: 4*

ZUCCHINI AU GRATIN

2 **MEDIUM ZUCCHINI**
2 **TABLESPOONS MARGARINE**
¼ **CUP DRY BREAD CRUMBS, PLUS FOR TOPPING**
½ **CAN CONDENSED CREAM OF MUSHROOM SOUP, UNDILUTED**
⅓ **CUP SHREDDED CHEDDAR OR AMERICAN CHEESE**
1 **TABLESPOON MINCED ONIONS SALT AND PEPPER TO TASTE**

Cut zucchini lengthwise and into slices ¼ inch thick. Melt 1 tablespoon margarine in a large skillet. Stir in bread crumbs. Toss and set aside.

Melt remaining margarine and sauté sliced squash 3-5 minutes. Add remaining ingredients to skillet and heat until cheese is melted. Serve topped with crumbs.

> *PREPARATION TIME: 10 MINUTES*
> *COOKING TIME: 10 MINUTES*
> *SERVES: 6*

ZUCCHINI WITH PESTO SAUCE

4 MEDIUM ZUCCHINI, JULIENNED
**   SALT TO TASTE**
¼ CUP OLIVE OIL

PESTO SAUCE:

**2 CUPS PACKED FRESH BASIL
   LEAVES**
3 CLOVES GARLIC
⅓ CUP PINE NUTS OR WALNUTS
**½ CUP OLIVE OIL. MORE IF
   DESIRED**
**½ CUP GRATED PARMESAN
   CHEESE**

Place zucchini in colander. Salt, toss, and drain for 20 minutes.

In a large skillet, sauté zucchini in oil until tender crisp. Add pesto sauce and toss to mix well.

Pesto Sauce:

Place basil, garlic, and nuts in a food processor or blender and pulverize leaves and nuts. Add oil and blend until mixture is smooth. Briefly blend in cheese.

Refrigerate until used. *Note:* Spinach or parsley may be substituted for basil.

> *PREPARATION TIME: 35 MINUTES*
> *COOKING TIME: 10 MINUTES*
> *SERVES: 4*

SUMMER SQUASH WITH LINGUINE PESTO

**4 MEDIUM SUMMER SQUASH,
   CUBED**
¼ CUP OLIVE OIL
4 SERVINGS LINGUINE
**½ CUP PESTO (SEE RECIPE ON
   PAGE 93)**
**   SLIVERED WALNUTS OR PINE
   NUTS (OPTIONAL)**

In a large skillet, sauté squash in oil until golden. Do not overcook. Squash should not get mushy.

In a large pot, cook pasta according to directions on package and drain. Return pasta to cooking pot and add pesto. Mix well. Serve pasta with squash and add slivered walnuts or pine nuts, if desired.

> *PREPARATION TIME: 15 MINUTES,
>   PLUS PESTO RECIPE*
> *COOKING TIME: 15 MINUTES*
> *SERVES: 4*

GARDEN MEDLEY

1 **MEDIUM ONION, MINCED**
1 **CLOVE GARLIC, MINCED**
3 **TABLESPOONS OLIVE OIL**
2 **MEDIUM BEETS, SLICED**
1 **MEDIUM GREEN PEPPER,**
   CHOPPED
2 **MEDIUM ZUCCHINI, SLICED**
2 **CUPS SHREDDED CABBAGE**
1 **MEDIUM TOMATO, PEELED AND**
   SEEDED
1 **TEASPOON DRIED ROSEMARY**
1 **TEASPOON DRIED THYME**
½ **CUP WATER**

Sauté onions and garlic in oil in a large deep skillet. Add remaining ingredients. Cover and simmer 20 minutes.

> *PREPARATION TIME: 10 MINUTES*
> *COOKING TIME: 20 MINUTES*
> *SERVES: 6*

SOUTH OF THE BORDER SQUASH

2 **CUPS SLICED ZUCCHINI**
2 **CUPS SLICED GOLDEN ZUCCHINI**
1 **MEDIUM ONION, MINCED**
2 **MEDIUM GREEN PEPPERS,**
   MINCED
¼ **CUP OLIVE OIL**
1 **MEDIUM TOMATO, PEELED AND**
   CHOPPED
2 **CUPS CORN**
½ **CUP WATER**
   SALT AND PEPPER TO TASTE

Sauté squash, onion, and peppers in oil until soft. Add tomato, corn, and water. Simmer 10-12 minutes. Season.

> *PREPARATION TIME: 10 MINUTES*
> *COOKING TIME: 10-12 MINUTES*
> *SERVES: 4-6*

ZUCCHINI PLUS YOGURT

3 MEDIUM ZUCCHINI, SLICED ¼
   INCH THICK
½ CUP OLIVE OIL
¼ TEASPOON SALT
¼ TEASPOON FRESHLY GROUND
   BLACK PEPPER
8 OUNCES LOW-FAT PLAIN
   YOGURT
½ TEASPOON GREEN ONION OR
   CHIVES

In a large skillet, sauté zucchini rounds in oil. Drain and season. Arrange on plates. In a small mixing bowl, combine remaining ingredients and spoon over zucchini.

PREPARATION TIME: 10 MINUTES
COOKING TIME: 5 MINUTES
SERVES: 4

ZUCCHINI SUCCOTASH

½ CUP OLIVE OIL
1 CLOVE GARLIC, MINCED
2 TABLESPOONS MINCED ONIONS
2 CUPS DICED ZUCCHINI
2 CUPS CORN
2 CUPS COOKED LIMA BEANS
1 MEDIUM GREEN PEPPER,
   MINCED
1 MEDIUM RED BELL PEPPER,
   MINCED
   SALT AND PEPPER TO TASTE
   PAPRIKA (OPTIONAL)

In a large skillet, heat oil and sauté garlic and onions. Add remaining ingredients. Season and simmer covered for 20 minutes. Sprinkle with paprika, if desired.

PREPARATION TIME: 15 MINUTES
COOKING TIME: 20 MINUTES
SERVES: 6

ZUCCHINI CURRY

2   **MEDIUM ONIONS, MINCED**
2   **CLOVES GARLIC, MINCED**
¼   **CUP MARGARINE**
2   **TEASPOONS CURRY POWDER**
1¼ **TEASPOONS GROUND CUMIN**
1   **TEASPOON SALT**
2   **CUPS DICED ZUCCHINI**
2   **CUPS SMALL CAULIFLOWER FLORETS**
1½ **CUPS CARROT ROUNDS**
1½ **CUPS CHICKEN BROTH OR BOUILLON**
1   **TABLESPOON LEMON JUICE**

In a large skillet, sauté onions and garlic in margarine. Add seasonings. Add remaining vegetables and broth. Cook 20 minutes. Add lemon juice.

PREPARATION TIME: 15 MINUTES
COOKING TIME: 20 MINUTES
SERVES: 4

ZUCCHINI "NOODLES"

6 **MEDIUM ZUCCHINI**
3 **TABLESPOONS BUTTER**
   SALT AND PEPPER TO TASTE
   PARMESAN CHEESE, GRATED

Cut zucchini lengthwise into narrow strips ⅛ inch thick. Melt butter in a large skillet. Add squash. Simmer until tender. Season and serve hot with cheese.

PREPARATION TIME: 10 MINUTES
COOKING TIME: 5 MINUTES
MAKES: 5 CUPS

SUMMER SQUASH AND PASTA

3 MEDIUM ZUCCHINI
3 MEDIUM YELLOW SUMMER
   SQUASH
2 LARGE CARROTS, PEELED
   WATER
4 TABLESPOONS BUTTER
2 SHALLOTS OR SMALL ONIONS,
   CHOPPED
1 CLOVE GARLIC, CHOPPED
   WATER
8-10 SERVINGS OF PASTA
2 TABLESPOONS BUTTER OR
   VEGETABLE OIL
   FRESH PARSLEY, MINCED
   SALT AND PEPPER TO TASTE

SAUCE:

1 TABLESPOON BUTTER OR
   VEGETABLE OIL
1 QUART CHICKEN OR VEAL
   BROTH
2 CUPS COOKED CUBED CHICKEN
1 TABLESPOON DRIED SAVORY

Cut squash into long narrow strips about ⅛ inch wide. Place in a large mixing bowl and cover. Cut carrots into long strips of similar size. In a small saucepan, blanch carrots in salted water for 2 minutes. Drain and refresh with cold water. Combine with squash and set aside.

Melt butter in a large skillet. Add shallots and garlic and sauté for 5 minutes. Add vegetable strips and sauté for 1-2 minutes. Set aside.

Bring salted water to a boil in a kettle and add pasta. Cook, while stirring for 2 minutes. Drain and return to kettle. Add warm vegetables to pasta. Toss mixture with 2 tablespoons butter or oil; season with parsley, salt, and pepper.

Prepare sauce and serve pasta with sauce.

PREPARATION TIME: 20 MINUTES
COOKING TIME: 15 MINUTES
SERVES: 8

SQUASH PILAF

⅓ **CUP OLIVE OIL**
1 **MEDIUM SUMMER SQUASH, CUBED**
1 **CUP BULGUR**
2 **CUPS CHICKEN BROTH**
⅓ **CUP GOLDEN RAISINS**
¾ **CUP RINSED AND DRAINED CHICK-PEAS**
SALT TO TASTE
FRESH PARSLEY, MINCED
PEPPER TO TASTE

Heat oil in a large saucepan. Add squash, tossing until lightly browned. Remove squash from oil and set aside.

Add bulgur and stir in oil until lightly browned. Add chicken broth, raisins, chick-peas and salt to taste.

Bring mixture to a boil, lower heat, cover, and simmer until liquid is absorbed. Sprinkle with parsley and pepper to taste.

PREPARATION TIME: 20 MINUTES
COOKING TIME: 10 MINUTES
SERVES: 2

STIR-FRY VEGETABLE STRIPS

½ **CUP THINLY SLICED GREEN PEPPER STRIPS**
½ **CUP THINLY SLICED CARROT STRIPS**
2 **TABLESPOONS VEGETABLE OIL**
½ **CUP CELERY STRIPS**
1 **MEDIUM ZUCCHINI, CUT INTO THIN STRIPS**
2 **TABLESPOONS CHICKEN BROTH**
6 **OUNCES SNOW PEAS**
SALT AND PEPPER TO TASTE

In a large skillet or wok, stir-fry green pepper and carrot strips in hot oil for 1 minute. Add celery and zucchini. Stir-fry 1 minute.

Add chicken broth. Cover and cook 30 seconds. Add snow peas and cook 1 minute more. Season.

PREPARATION TIME: 10 MINUTES
COOKING TIME: 5 MINUTES
SERVES: 6

ZUCCHINI-CABBAGE STIR-FRY

3 TABLESPOONS VEGETABLE OIL
1 CLOVE GARLIC, MINCED
3 CUPS THINLY SLICED ZUCCHINI
4 CUPS GRATED CABBAGE
1 MEDIUM ONION, THINLY
   SLICED
2 TEASPOONS SALT
1 TEASPOON SUGAR
   PEPPER TO TASTE
   CELERY SEED TO TASTE

Heat oil in a large skillet or wok. Add garlic. Brown garlic and discard. Add vegetables and stir-fry 2-3 minutes.

Add seasonings. Reduce heat and continue stirring 5-6 minutes until vegetables are cooked, but still crisp.

PREPARATION TIME: 15 MINUTES
COOKING TIME: 10 MINUTES
SERVES: 6

ZUCCHINI CUPS STUFFED WITH PUREE

3 OR 4 MEDIUM ZUCCHINI
½ TABLESPOON OLIVE OIL
1 SLICE STALE BREAD, CUBED
1 EGG, PLUS 1 EGG YOLK
½ TEASPOON SALT
1 TABLESPOON DRIED BASIL
   PEPPER TO TASTE
   GROUND NUTMEG TO TASTE
   WATER

Preheat oven to 350°F. Cut four 2-inch rounds from the middle of the zucchini. Scoop out each piece to make a serving cup, leaving a ¾-inch base and ¼-inch thickness in the side of each piece. Reserve pulp. Invert shells on paper towels to drain. Chop reserved pulp and heat in oil for 20 minutes to evaporate moisture. Do not brown.

In a food processor or blender, combine pulp, bread, egg, extra yolk, and seasonings. Blend or process until smooth. Fill drained squash cups with mixture.

Place filled cups in a baking dish, add ¼-inch water, and cover with aluminum foil. Bake 30 minutes at 350°F. Uncover and continue baking for another 20 minutes.

PREPARATION TIME: 30 MINUTES
BAKING TIME: 50 MINUTES TOTAL
SERVES: 4

STUFFED ZUCCHINI MORNAY

2 TABLESPOONS MARGARINE
2 TABLESPOONS ALL-PURPOSE
　FLOUR
1 CUP MILK
1 EGG YOLK
2 TABLESPOONS CREAM
2 TABLESPOONS GRATED
　GRUYÈRE CHEESE
　SALT AND PEPPER TO TASTE
3 MEDIUM ZUCCHINI
　WATER
½ CUP MINCED ONIONS
2 TABLESPOONS MARGARINE
½ CUP MINCED COOKED HAM *or*
　CRUMBLED BACON BITS
2 TABLESPOONS GRATED
　PARMESAN CHEESE

Preheat oven to 400°F. Make a sauce in a large saucepan by melting margarine and adding flour. Cook for 3 minutes, stirring. Add milk and mix well. In a small mixing bowl, beat egg yolk and cream together. Add 2 tablespoons of sauce. Combine this mixture with remaining sauce in the saucepan and stir until heated through. Add Gruyère cheese and stir until melted.

Cut zucchini in half lengthwise and blanch in boiling water 5 minutes. Drain. Scoop out pulp and add it to onions, margarine, and ham. Combine with sauce and season to taste.

Fill zucchini shells, sprinkle with Parmesan cheese, and bake at 400°F. until cheese is melted.

PREPARATION TIME: 30 MINUTES
COOKING TIME: 20 MINUTES
SERVES: 6

ZUCCHINI BOATS WITH CHEESE

2 MEDIUM ZUCCHINI, CUT IN HALF
　LENGTHWISE
　WATER
2 MEDIUM TOMATOES, CHOPPED
1½ CUPS GRATED CHEDDAR
　CHEESE
4 STRIPS BACON, PARTIALLY
　COOKED
　DRY BREAD CRUMBS, SEASONED

Place zucchini in water to cover and parboil in a large saucepan. Drain and remove seeds.

In a medium mixing bowl, combine tomatoes and cheese and stuff squash. Include some pulp.

Top squash with a strip of bacon. Broil until bacon is crisp. Sprinkle with bread crumbs and serve hot.

PREPARATION TIME: 15 MINUTES
COOKING TIME: 10 MINUTES
SERVES: 4

STUFFED SUMMER SQUASH

6 MEDIUM ZUCCHINI
3 CLOVES GARLIC, MINCED
1 CUP CHOPPED MUSHROOMS
1 CUP CHOPPED WALNUTS
3 TABLESPOONS SWEET BUTTER
¼ TEASPOON DRIED OREGANO
½ CUP FRESH BREAD CRUMBS
   SALT AND PEPPER TO TASTE
1 CUP GRATED MILD CHEDDAR
   CHEESE

Preheat oven to 350°F. Halve zucchini lengthwise. Remove pulp and chop. Set aside.

Sauté in butter, the garlic, mushrooms, and walnuts in a large skillet. Add chopped zucchini and oregano. Cook slowly, while stirring for 8 minutes. Set mixture aside and allow to cool.

Stir in bread crumbs, salt, and pepper. Divide mixture among the twelve zucchini shells. Place shells in a large buttered baking dish and sprinkle with cheese. Bake for 25 minutes. Pierce with fork to assure tenderness.

PREPARATION TIME: 30 MINUTES
BAKING TIME: 25 MINUTES
SERVES: 12

STUFFED PATTYPAN

6 MEDIUM PATTYPAN SQUASH
6 STRIPS BACON
1 MEDIUM ONION, MINCED
2 CLOVES GARLIC, MINCED
1 CUP DRY BREAD CRUMBS
1 TABLESPOON MINCED FRESH
   PARSLEY
¼ TEASPOON DRIED BASIL
¼ TEASPOON DRIED TARRAGON
¼ TEASPOON DRIED ROSEMARY
   SALT AND PEPPER TO TASTE
½ CUP CHICKEN BROTH OR
   BOUILLON

Preheat oven to 350°F. Cut thin lids from squash. In a large saucepan, blanch squash and lids 10-15 minutes until tender. Scoop pulp from squash and chop. Turn squash upside down to drain.

In a large skillet, sauté bacon, drain and crumble. Saute onion and garlic in bacon drippings. Pour off excess grease. Add bread crumbs, squash pulp, and seasonings. Simmer 5 minutes.

Add crumbled bacon. Butter squash cases and stuff with mixture. Place squash in a large shallow baking dish. Add broth. Top squash with lids. Bake about 20 minutes.

PREPARATION TIME: 20 MINUTES
BAKING TIME: 20 MINUTES
SERVES: 6

WHEAT GERM STUFFED ZUCCHINI

4 SMALL ZUCCHINI
2 TABLESPOONS CHOPPED
   ONIONS
1 TABLESPOON MARGARINE
½ CUP SEASONED STUFFING
¼ CUP TOASTED WHEAT GERM
1 SMALL TOMATO, PEELED AND
   CHOPPED
¼ CUP GRATED PARMESAN
   CHEESE

Preheat oven to 350°F. In a large saucepan, blanch zucchini until barely tender. Cut in half lengthwise. Scoop out pulp and chop.

In a large skillet, brown onions in margarine. Add zucchini pulp to stuffing, wheat germ, and tomato. Add mixture to the skillet and simmer until reduced.

Stuff shells and sprinkle with cheese. Bake until cheese melts, about 8-10 minutes.

PREPARATION TIME: 25 MINUTES
BAKING TIME: 8-10 MINUTES
SERVES: 4

FRUIT FILLED WINTER SQUASH

2 MEDIUM ACORN OR OTHER
   WINTER SQUASH
   WATER
4 EACH DRIED APPLES, APRICOTS,
   PEACHES, AND PRUNES (OR AN
   EQUAL AMOUNT OF 2)
2 TABLESPOONS HONEY OR
   SUGAR SYRUP

Preheat oven to 350°F. Cut squashes in half and remove lids. Simmer, cut side down, in 1-inch water in a large covered skillet until tender.

Chop fruit. In a large saucepan, simmer fruit with sweetener. Fill squash halves. Heat in oven until warmed through, about 10 minutes. *Note:* Fresh fruit may be used by combining 1 cup orange sections, 1 tablespoon grated orange peel, ½ cup grapefruit sections, and 2 tablespoons raisins with brown sugar in a buttered cooked squash half. Bake 15 minutes at 375°F.

PREPARATION TIME: 20 MINUTES
COOKING TIME: 10 MINUTES
SERVES: 4

ACORN SQUASH FILLED WITH MIXED VEGETABLES

1 MEDIUM ACORN SQUASH, CUT IN
   HALF LENGTHWISE

1 CUP MIXED VEGETABLES
   (SUCCOTASH; PEAS AND
   CARROTS; GREEN PEPPER,
   CELERY, AND CORN; PEAS,
   ONIONS, AND MUSHROOMS;
   ETC.)

½ CUP WHITE SAUCE OR
   3 TABLESPOONS LOW-FAT
   PLAIN YOGURT

3 TABLESPOONS LOW-CALORIE
   MAYONNAISE (OPTIONAL)

2 TABLESPOONS BUTTERMILK
   (OPTIONAL)
   FRESHLY CHOPPED HERBS
   (OPTIONAL)
   GARLIC SALT (OPTIONAL)

Bake squash as in *Fruit Filled Winter Squash.* Fill with mixed vegetables and white sauce or a more piquant sauce made by combining the remaining optional ingredients.

PREPARATION TIME: 20 MINUTES
COOKING TIME: 20 MINUTES
SERVES: 2

SQUASH WITH SCALLOPED ONIONS

1 **MEDIUM ACORN SQUASH, CUT IN HALF LENGTHWISE**
SALT
1 **CUP CHOPPED ONIONS**
WATER
2 **TABLESPOONS MARGARINE**
1 **TABLESPOON ALL-PURPOSE FLOUR**
½ **CUP MILK**
GROUND NUTMEG TO TASTE

Preheat oven to 350°F. Remove seeds from squash halves and place cut side down on a baking sheet. Bake for 45 minutes. With fork loosen pulp a little and salt well.

In a small saucepan, cook onions in boiling salted water until tender. Drain.

In a small saucepan, melt margarine. Stir in flour and gradually add milk until thick. Combine with onions and pour into squash halves. Sprinkle with nutmeg and return to oven for 15 minutes.

> *PREPARATION TIME: 20 MINUTES*
> *COOKING TIME: 1 HOUR TOTAL*
> *SERVES: 2*

ZUCCHINI STRATA

3 **CUPS SLICED ZUCCHINI**
WATER
4 **SLICES CRACKED WHEAT BREAD**
8 **OUNCES SHARP CHEESE, SHREDDED**
2 **TABLESPOONS MELTED MARGARINE**
3 **EGGS, BEATEN**
¼ **CUP MINCED ONIONS**
½ **TEASPOON SALT**
½ **TEASPOON DRY MUSTARD**
CAYENNE PEPPER TO TASTE
1½ **CUPS MILK**

Preheat oven to 350°F. In a large saucepan, cook zucchini in boiling salted water about 5 minutes. Drain and pat dry.

Line a well-greased 9-inch baking pan with bread slices. In a large mixing bowl, combine zucchini with cheese and margarine. Spread over bread.

In a large mixing bowl, beat remaining ingredients and pour over zucchini mix. Refrigerate 1 hour. Bake until puffed, set, and browned, about 40-50 minutes.

> *PREPARATION TIME: 1 HOUR 15 MINUTES*
> *BAKING TIME: 40-50 MINUTES*
> *SERVES: 4*

PUMPKIN TEMPURA

1 POUND PUMPKIN OR WINTER SQUASH, PEELED AND CUT INTO BITE-SIZED CUBES
1 CUP ALL-PURPOSE FLOUR
⅓ TEASPOON SUGAR
⅓ TEASPOON SALT
⅓ TEASPOON GROUND CINNAMON
PINCH GROUND NUTMEG
1 EGG, BEATEN
2 TABLESPOONS VEGETABLE OIL
HOT OIL

Dip cubed pumpkin into a batter of combined flour, sugar, salt, cinnamon, nutmeg, egg, and vegetable oil. Deep-fry in hot oil until golden brown. Drain on paper towels and serve hot.

PREPARATION TIME: 10 MINUTES
COOKING TIME: 5 MINUTES
SERVES: 4

ZUCCHINI TEMPURA

6 CUPS ZUCCHINI, SLICED IN ½-INCH STRIPS
SALT AND PEPPER TO TASTE
⅓ CUP ALL-PURPOSE FLOUR
2 EGGS, BEATEN AND DILUTED WITH ⅓ CUP MILK
⅓ CUP DRY BREAD CRUMBS
HOT OIL

Dredge zucchini strips in seasoned flour. Dip into egg mixture and then into bread crumbs. Spread strips on a baking sheet and chill thoroughly.

At serving time, fry zucchini in hot oil until browned. Drain briefly on paper towels and serve immediately.

PREPARATION TIME: 10 MINUTES
COOKING TIME: 5 MINUTES
SERVES: 6

CHAPTER 8

SPAGHETTI SQUASH

Spaghetti squash, a novel cucurbit which fascinates cooks and dieters, frequently is called "vegetable spaghetti." This squash is easy to grow and adapts well to most pasta recipes. Its fibrous consistency provides a product which roughly resembles true spaghetti.

This vegetable spaghetti has one very decided advantage over pasta. It has a very low caloric value and is a weight-watcher's dream.

Spaghetti squash is easily prepared. Make five or six deep punctures in the skin. Boil squash whole or bake in a conventional oven at 350°F. until the skin begins to give. For the microwave, puncture squash, place on paper towel and microwave on high for six minutes. Turn squash completely over and microwave for another six minutes.

Note: All of the recipes and times in this section are for the preparation of *precooked* spaghetti squash.

See chapter 5 for spaghetti squash salad recipe.

SPAGHETTI SQUASH BAKE

2   TABLESPOONS MARGARINE
2⅓ TABLESPOONS ALL-PURPOSE
     FLOUR
1   TEASPOON SALT
1⅓ CUPS MILK
1   CUP COOKED, DRAINED, AND
     CHOPPED SPINACH
½   TEASPOON GROUND NUTMEG
1½ CUPS COOKED SPAGHETTI
     SQUASH
½   CUP COTTAGE CHEESE
2   HARD-BOILED EGGS, SLICED
     PARMESAN CHEESE, GRATED

Preheat oven to 350°F. Make a white sauce by melting margarine in a small saucepan, then adding flour and salt. Add milk gradually and stir until thick.

In a medium mixing bowl, combine 1 cup of the white sauce with spinach and nutmeg. Into a well-greased 1-quart casserole, pour the remaining sauce.

Layer the spinach mixture, squash, cottage cheese, and egg slices. Sprinkle with Parmesan cheese. Bake for 30 minutes.

> PREPARATION TIME: 15 MINUTES
> BAKING TIME: 30 MINUTES
> SERVES: 2

AL BURRO

2 CUPS COOKED SPAGHETTI SQUASH
BUTTER, MELTED
GARLIC SALT TO TASTE
PARMESAN CHEESE, GRATED

Simply toss cooked spaghetti squash with melted butter (burro), garlic salt, and freshly grated Parmesan.

> PREPARATION TIME: 10 MINUTES
> SERVES: 2

SAUTÉED SPAGHETTI SQUASH

WATER
1 MEDIUM SPAGHETTI SQUASH
2 TABLESPOONS OLIVE OIL
1 TABLESPOON BUTTER
¼ TEASPOON DRIED BASIL
¼ TEASPOON DRIED OREGANO
   SALT AND PEPPER TO TASTE
2½ TABLESPOONS LEMON JUICE
½ POUND FETA CHEESE,
   CRUMBLED
3 EGGS, HARD-BOILED AND
   QUARTERED
½ SMALL RED ONION, THINLY
   SLICED
   FRESH PARSLEY, CHOPPED

In a large saucepan, bring water to a boil. Add whole squash. Reduce heat, cover, and simmer 30 minutes. Drain and cool squash. Cut squash in half lengthwise and remove seeds. Loosen strands of "spaghetti" with a fork.

Heat oil and butter in a medium skillet. Add "spaghetti" and seasonings and heat 5 minutes.

Transfer to a serving platter. Sprinkle with lemon juice. Arrange cheese, eggs, onions, and parsley around and on top of squash. Serve hot.

> *PREPARATION TIME: 30 MINUTES*
> *COOKING TIME: 35 MINUTES*
> *SERVES: 4*

SPAGHETTI SQUASH PIE

4 CUPS COOKED SPAGHETTI
   SQUASH
1 8-OUNCE CAN TOMATO SAUCE
1 TABLESPOON TOMATO PASTE
½ CUP GRATED ROMANO CHEESE
½ POUND GROUND BEEF, COOKED
1 UNBAKED 9-INCH PIE SHELL
2 EGGS
   PINCH DRIED OREGANO
   SALT AND PEPPER TO TASTE

Preheat oven to 350°F. In a large mixing bowl, mix cooked spaghetti squash with tomato sauce, tomato paste, cheese, and cooked beef. Place in the pie shell.

Beat eggs and pour over squash mixture. Add seasonings. Bake for 25 minutes.

> *PREPARATION TIME: 15 MINUTES*
> *BAKING TIME: 25 MINUTES*
> *SERVES: 4*

VARIED SAUCES

Prepare squash as explained in the introduction to chapter 8.
Serve with one of the following sauces:

ITALIAN

1 CLOVE GARLIC, MINCED
½ POUND GROUND BEEF
¼ POUND PORK SAUSAGE
½ CUP OLIVE OIL
2 CUPS PEELED AND CHOPPED
    TOMATOES
½ CUP TOMATO PASTE
½ CUP BEEF BROTH OR BOUILLON
¼ TEASPOON DRIED OREGANO
    SALT AND PEPPER TO TASTE

In a large skillet, sauté garlic and ground meats in oil until cooked, but not browned. Add remaining ingredients and mix thoroughly. Simmer over low heat for 1 hour.

PREPARATION TIME: 10 MINUTES
COOKING TIME: 1 HOUR
SERVES: 4

MEDITERRANEAN

2 TABLESPOONS OLIVE OIL
1 TABLESPOON BUTTER
¼ TEASPOON DRIED BASIL
    SALT AND PEPPER TO TASTE
2 TABLESPOONS LEMON JUICE
½ POUND FETA CHEESE, DICED
    SPAGHETTI SQUASH, COOKED
3 EGGS, HARD-BOILED AND
    QUARTERED
1 2-OUNCE CAN ANCHOVIES,
    DRAINED
    FRESH PARSLEY, CHOPPED

In a small saucepan, heat olive oil and butter. Add seasonings and lemon juice. Mix well. Add feta cheese and stir mixture until cheese begins to melt.
   Pour sauce over prepared squash. Garnish with eggs and anchovies. Sprinkle with fresh parsley.

PREPARATION TIME: 20 MINUTES
COOKING TIME: 10 MINUTES
SERVES: 4

MILANESE

2 SLICES BACON, COOKED AND
   CRUMBLED
1 MEDIUM ONION, DICED
1 CLOVE GARLIC, MINCED
1 CARROT, MINCED
⅛ TEASPOON DRIED THYME
2 CUPS PEELED AND CHOPPED
   TOMATOES
2 TABLESPOONS TOMATO PASTE
2 CUPS CHICKEN BROTH OR
   WATER
½ CUP COOKED CHOPPED HAM
1 4-OUNCE CAN MUSHROOM
   PIECES
   SALT AND PEPPER TO TASTE
   SPAGHETTI SQUASH, COOKED

In a large skillet, cook bacon, drain, and set aside. In drippings, sauté onion, garlic, and carrot until tender.

Add next four ingredients and simmer for 1 hour or more until mixture reaches sauce consistency. Add ham and mushrooms to sauce, season, and serve over cooked spaghetti squash.

> *PREPARATION TIME: 15 MINUTES*
> *COOKING TIME: 1 HOUR*
> *SERVES: 4*

SEAFOOD

½ CUP CHOPPED ONIONS
1 CLOVE GARLIC, MINCED
1 TABLESPOON MELTED
   MARGARINE
1 TABLESPOON OLIVE OIL
3 CUPS PEELED AND SEEDED
   TOMATOES
1 TABLESPOON TOMATO PASTE
¼ TEASPOON DRIED OREGANO
2 CUPS SMALL SHRIMP, TUNA,
   CRAB, LOBSTER, CLAMS, OR
   OYSTERS
   SALT AND PEPPER TO TASTE
   SPAGHETTI SQUASH, COOKED

In a large skillet, sauté onions and garlic in margarine and oil. Add remaining ingredients, except seafood, and simmer, stirring frequently for 20 minutes.

Add seafood, correct seasoning, and simmer for 5-7 minutes. Serve over cooked spaghetti squash.

> *PREPARATION TIME: 20 MINUTES*
> *COOKING TIME: 25 MINUTES*
> *SERVES: 4*

HAM AND ZUCCHINI

3 TABLESPOONS VEGETABLE OIL
1 SMALL ONION, CHOPPED
2 CLOVES GARLIC, MINCED
2 MEDIUM ZUCCHINI, THINLY
   SLICED
1 CUP COOKED CUBED HAM
½ CUP LOW-FAT PLAIN YOGURT
   SPAGHETTI SQUASH, COOKED
2 TABLESPOONS GRATED
   PARMESAN CHEESE

In a large skillet, heat oil, add onion and garlic, and sauté slowly until liquid is almost evaporated.

Add zucchini and cook until soft. Add ham and sauté for 2 minutes. Add yogurt and heat sauce thoroughly.

Serve over cooked spaghetti squash. Sprinkle with cheese.

PREPARATION TIME: 20 MINUTES
COOKING TIME: 10 MINUTES
SERVES: 4

SPAGHETTI SQUASH WITH CHICKEN LIVERS

½ POUND CHICKEN LIVERS
   GARLIC SALT TO TASTE
¼ CUP OLIVE OIL
1 SMALL ONION, MINCED
½ CUP DRY WHITE WINE
1½ CUPS COOKED SPAGHETTI
   SQUASH
2 BAKED SPAGHETTI SQUASH
   HALVES

Preheat over to 350°F. Season livers with garlic salt. In a large skillet, sauté livers in oil, but do not brown. Drain and set aside. Add onion and sauté until translucent.

Chop livers and combine with onions, wine, and squash into baked squash halves. Heat thoroughly in oven for 15-20 minutes.

PREPARATION TIME: 20 MINUTES
COOKING TIME: 15-20 MINUTES
SERVES: 4

SPAGHETTI SQUASH CHEESE BAKE

4 SLICES BACON, COOKED AND
    CRUMBLED
1 8-OUNCE PACKAGE GRATED
    CHEDDAR CHEESE
    SALT AND PEPPER TO TASTE
1½ CUPS COOKED SPAGHETTI
    SQUASH

Preheat oven to 325°F. In a large mixing bowl, combine all ingredients with fluffed-up spaghetti squash. Place mixture in a baking dish and heat in oven until cheese melts, about 5 minutes.

> *PREPARATION TIME: 10 MINUTES*
> *COOKING TIME: 5 MINUTES*
> *SERVES: 2*

VEGETABLE SPAGHETTI

3 TABLESPOONS OLIVE OIL
1 CUP CHOPPED ONIONS
1 CUP DICED CELERY
1 CUP CHOPPED GREEN
    PEPPERS
1 SMALL CARROT, DICED
1 CLOVE GARLIC, CHOPPED
1½ POUNDS TOMATOES, PEELED
    AND CHOPPED
2 TABLESPOONS TOMATO PASTE
1 BAY LEAF
    COARSE BLACK PEPPER, DRIED
    OREGANO, DRIED BASIL, AND
    SALT TO TASTE
1 CUP CHOPPED ZUCCHINI
    SPAGHETTI SQUASH, COOKED
    PARMESAN CHEESE, GRATED

Place all ingredients except the last three in a large covered skillet. Simmer 45 minutes.

Add zucchini and cook for 15 minutes more. Spoon over spaghetti squash and sprinkle with cheese. *Note:* Sautéed mushrooms may be added just before serving.

> *PREPARATION TIME: 20 MINUTES*
> *COOKING TIME: 1 HOUR TOTAL*
> *SERVES: 4*

CRÊPES

These are thin pancakes onto which a tablespoon of filling is placed. They are then rolled up and served warm with a light sauce such as a béchamel or mornay (see "The Sauce Recipes" page 28.)

BASIC BATTER

¾   CUP ALL-PURPOSE FLOUR
1   CUP SKIM MILK
1   EGG, SLIGHTLY BEATEN
1   TABLESPOON MELTED
     MARGARINE

Beat all ingredients together in a blender. Let stand 20 minutes. Thin if necessary.

Pour 2 tablespoons batter into a well-greased 6-inch skillet, moderately heated. Tilt pan to spread. Cook until golden brown on each side.

They may be frozen for later use. Fill these crêpes with one of the fillings below. The crêpes may be the main dish for any meal.

WHOLE-WHEAT BATTER

1   CUP WHOLE-WHEAT FLOUR
1½   CUPS MILK
2   EGGS
1   TABLESPOON VEGETABLE OIL
¼   TEASPOON SALT

PREPARATION TIME: 25 MINUTES
COOKING TIME: VARIABLE
MAKES: 12-14

ZUCCHINI FILLING

2 **CUPS THINLY SLICED SQUASH**
1 **CUP CHOPPED ONIONS**
½ **CUP CHOPPED GREEN PEPPERS**
3 **CLOVES GARLIC, MINCED**
2 **TABLESPOONS OLIVE OIL**
1 **16-OUNCE CAN TOMATO SAUCE**
½ **CUP COTTAGE OR RICOTTA CHEESE**
½ **CUP GRATED PARMESAN CHEESE**

In a large skillet, sauté squash, onions, green peppers, and garlic in oil until tender. Add tomato sauce and cook for 10 minutes. Add cheeses and mix well.

PREPARATION TIME: 10 MINUTES
COOKING TIME: 10 MINUTES
MAKES: 4 CUPS

CREAM SOUP FILLING

2 **CUPS CHOPPED ZUCCHINI**
6 **TABLESPOONS CHOPPED ONIONS**
3 **TABLESPOONS MELTED MARGARINE**
1 **CAN CONDENSED CREAM OF CHICKEN OR SHRIMP SOUP, UNDILUTED**
¼ **CUP MILK**

In a medium skillet, sauté zucchini and onions in margarine until soft. Stir in soup and milk.

PREPARATION TIME: 5 MINUTES
COOKING TIME: 10 MINUTES
MAKES: 3 CUPS

HAM FILLING

¼ **CUP CHOPPED ONIONS**
¼ **CUP CHOPPED CELERY**
¼ **CUP CHOPPED FRESH**
    MUSHROOMS
½ **CUP CHOPPED ZUCCHINI**
2 **TABLESPOONS MARGARINE**
¾ **CUP COOKED CHOPPED HAM OR**
    BACON
1 **CUP BÉCHAMEL SAUCE (SEE**
    PAGE 28)

In a large skillet, sauté vegetables in margarine. Add cooked meat. Stir in béchamel sauce. Chicken broth may be substituted for the milk and 3 tablespoons grated cheese may be added. *Note:* This is a creative and attractive way to serve leftovers.

PREPARATION TIME: 10 MINUTES
COOKING TIME: 10 MINUTES
MAKES: ALMOST 3 CUPS

BACON FILLING

¼ **CUP CHOPPED CELERY**
¼ **CUP CHOPPED ONIONS**
½ **CUP CHOPPED ZUCCHINI**
2 **TABLESPOONS MARGARINE**
4 **STRIPS BACON, COOKED AND**
    CRUMBLED
1 **CUP BÉCHAMEL SAUCE (SEE**
    PAGE 28)

In a large skillet, sauté vegetables in margarine. Add cooked meat. Stir in béchamel sauce. Chicken broth may be substituted for the milk and 3 tablespoons grated cheese may be added. *Note:* This is a creative and attractive way to serve leftovers.

PREPARATION TIME: 10 MINUTES
COOKING TIME: 10 MINUTES
MAKES: ALMOST 3 CUPS

SOUR CREAM FILLING

1½ **CUPS GRATED AND DRAINED ZUCCHINI**
2 **TABLESPOONS MELTED MARGARINE**
1½ **CUPS SOUR CREAM**
1½ **CUPS GRATED PARMESAN CHEESE**

In a medium skillet, sauté zucchini in margarine until tender. Stir in sour cream and cheese.

> *PREPARATION TIME: 5 MINUTES*
> *COOKING TIME: 10 MINUTES*
> *MAKES: 4 CUPS*

CUSTARDS

Custard is usually thought of as a type of dessert. This is not necessarily the case. Similar to a quiche, an unsweetened custard is a very suitable base for a vegetable dish. The following recipe is an example. A recipe for a dessert type of custard made with pumpkin is in the chapter on desserts.

ZUCCHINI-RICE CUSTARD

4 **SMALL ZUCCHINI, THINLY SLICED**
WATER
⅓ **CUP DRIED PARSLEY**
¼ **CUP COOKED RICE**
⅓ **CUP ALL-PURPOSE FLOUR**
½ **TEASPOON SALT**
⅛ **TEASPOON CAYENNE PEPPER**
1 **EGG**
¼ **CUP SOUR CREAM**
½ **CUP GRATED PARMESAN CHEESE**
2 **TABLESPOONS MARGARINE**

Preheat oven to 375°F. In a medium saucepan, cook zucchini in a small amount of boiling salted water until tender. Drain. Arrange one-half the zucchini in a well-greased 1-quart baking dish. Layer with parsley and rice. Shake remaining zucchini with the flour and place over rice.

Stir together the next four ingredients and one-half the cheese. (A scant cup of milk may replace the sour cream.) Pour custard mixture over all. Dot with margarine and sprinkle with remaining cheese. Bake for 40 minutes, or until set.

> *PREPARATION TIME: 5 MINUTES*
> *BAKING TIME: 40 MINUTES*
> *SERVES: 4*

ZUCCHINI CUSTARD PUDDING

1   MEDIUM ZUCCHINI, GRATED
1   TABLESPOON SALT
4   EGGS
½   CUP MILK OR CREAM
¾   CUP FINE DRY BREAD CRUMBS
½   TEASPOON DRIED OREGANO
3   TABLESPOONS GRATED
       PARMESAN CHEESE
2   TABLESPOONS MELTED
       MARGARINE

Preheat oven to 350°F. Sprinkle grated zucchini with salt and drain. Before using, squeeze out as much moisture as possible.

In a medium mixing bowl, beat eggs, add milk, bread crumbs, seasoning, cheese, and margarine. Fold in zucchini. Pour into a well-greased 1-quart baking dish. Bake for 40 minutes.

PREPARATION TIME: 10 MINUTES
BAKING TIME: 40 MINUTES
SERVES: 4

OMELETTES

Like the soufflé, the omelette and its idiosyncracies often strike terror in the heart of a neophyte cook. Some people refuse to meet the challenge and stick to scrambled eggs. There isn't much taste difference; the primary distinctions are texture and appearance.

If the thought of making an omelette throws you, so what? Scramble up some eggs and serve them with a delicious squash filling and who will know the difference? Frittatas are omelette cousins.

ZUCCHINI OMELETTE

1	**MEDIUM ZUCCHINI, THINLY SLICED**
1	**MEDIUM ONION, SLICED**
1½	**TABLESPOONS OLIVE OIL**
2	**TABLESPOONS WATER**
½	**TEASPOON FRESH BASIL**
¾	**CUP SHREDDED MILD CHEESE**
	PARMESAN CHEESE, GRATED
4	**EGGS**

In a medium saucepan, simmer zucchini and onion in oil and water until tender. Combine with basil and shredded cheese.

Place this mixture inside a prepared 4-egg omelette. Sprinkle with Parmesan cheese.

PREPARATION TIME: 10 MINUTES
COOKING TIME: 10 MINUTES
SERVES: 2

SPANISH SQUASH OMELETTE

1 **MEDIUM ZUCCHINI, THINLY SLICED**
2 **TABLESPOONS DICED GREEN PEPPERS**
1 **TABLESPOON DICED ONIONS**
1 **TABLESPOON OLIVE OIL**
1 **TOMATO, PEELED, SEEDED, AND DICED**
   DASH TABASCO SAUCE
   SALT AND PEPPER TO TASTE
1 **8-OUNCE CAN TOMATO SAUCE**
   4 EGGS

In a medium skillet, sauté zucchini, green peppers, and onions in oil. Add tomato, Tabasco, seasonings, and one-half the tomato sauce. Simmer 10 minutes.

Prepare 4-egg omelette. Remove to platter. Place filling on one-half of omelette. Fold and serve with additional sauce.

> *PREPARATION TIME: 10 MINUTES*
> *COOKING TIME: 15 MINUTES*
> *SERVES: 2*

LOW CHOLESTEROL SQUASH FRITTATA

1   **EGG**
5   **EGG WHITES**
2   **TABLESPOONS GRATED PARMESAN CHEESE**
1   **TABLESPOON FRESH PARSLEY**
¼   **TEASPOON DRIED BASIL**
⅛   **TEASPOON FRESHLY GROUND BLACK PEPPER**
     OLIVE OIL COOKING SPRAY
1   **CUP CHOPPED ZUCCHINI**
½   **CUP CHOPPED FRESH MUSHROOMS**
¼   **CUP SLICED GREEN ONIONS**
1   **CLOVE GARLIC, MINCED**
½   **CUP GRATED LOW-FAT MOZZARELLA CHEESE**

Preheat oven to 350°F. In a small mixing bowl, lightly beat whole egg and whites together. Add Parmesan cheese and seasonings. Spray a medium skillet with olive oil spray and stir-fry zucchini, mushrooms, onions, and garlic until tender.

Remove from heat and pour in egg mixture. Transfer to a well-greased baking dish, and bake uncovered until eggs are set.

Sprinkle mozzarella on top and continue baking until cheese is melted. Slice frittata into serving pieces.

> *PREPARATION TIME: 25 MINUTES*
> *COOKING TIME: 15 MINUTES*
> *SERVES: 3*

CORN AND SQUASH FRITTATA

3 EARS FRESH CORN
2 EGGS, BEATEN
2 TABLESPOONS ALL-PURPOSE
   FLOUR
¼ TEASPOON BAKING POWDER
¼ TEASPOON SALT
¼ TEASPOON FRESHLY GROUND
   BLACK PEPPER
1 MEDIUM SUMMER SQUASH,
   GRATED
   COOKING SPRAY
1½ TABLESPOONS BUTTER
   FRESH PARSLEY

Cut kernels from cob and set aside. In a medium mixing bowl, combine eggs, flour, baking powder, salt, and pepper. Whisk mixture. Add reserved corn and squash and mix well.

Spray skillet with cooking spray and melt butter. Add egg mixture. Cover skillet and cook frittata slowly until set. Sprinkle with parsley. Cut into serving pieces.

> *PREPARATION TIME: 15 MINUTES*
> *COOKING TIME: 15 MINUTES*
> *SERVES: 4*

PANCAKES AND WAFFLES

Ever have squash or pumpkin for breakfast? There is no time like the present. Tired of your old pancake recipe? Surprise your family and friends at breakfast, brunch, and supper, too, with a different kind of pancake or waffle.

ZUCCHINI PANCAKES

1 MEDIUM ZUCCHINI, GRATED
   AND DRAINED
1 EGG, BEATEN
1 TABLESPOON VEGETABLE OIL
1 CUP PANCAKE MIX
¾ CUP MILK
2 TABLESPOONS GRATED
   PARMESAN CHEESE

In a medium mixing bowl, lightly combine all ingredients and allow to rest for 30 minutes. Add more milk for a thinner pancake. Cook on a lightly greased, hot griddle.

> *PREPARATION TIME: 40 MINUTES*
> *COOKING TIME: 10 MINUTES*
> *SERVES: 2-3*

PUMPKIN WAFFLES

2 CUPS ALL-PURPOSE FLOUR
2 TEASPOONS BAKING POWDER
¼ TEASPOON GROUND
   CINNAMON
¼ TEASPOON GROUND GINGER
¼ TEASPOON GROUND NUTMEG
½ TEASPOON SALT
3 EGGS, BEATEN
1¾ CUPS MILK
½ CUP VEGETABLE OIL
¾ CUP COOKED AND MASHED
   PUMPKIN
½ CUP CHOPPED NUTS

In a large mixing bowl, sift dry ingredients together. Mix well with eggs, milk, oil, and pumpkin.

Stir in nuts. Bake in a hot waffle iron. *Note:* Whole-wheat flour may be substituted.

PREPARATION TIME: 15 MINUTES
COOKING TIME: 15 MINUTES
SERVES: 4

ZUCCHINI-CARROT-POTATO CAKE

1 MEDIUM ZUCCHINI, COARSELY
   SHREDDED AND SQUEEZED
   DRY
1 LARGE CARROT, COARSELY
   SHREDDED
2 LARGE POTATOES, COARSELY
   SHREDDED AND SQUEEZED
   DRY
1 MEDIUM ONION, FINELY
   CHOPPED
3 EGGS, LIGHTLY BEATEN
¼ CUP OAT BRAN FLOUR
1 TEASPOON SALT
¼ TEASPOON DRIED BASIL
¼ TEASPOON FRESHLY GROUND
   BLACK PEPPER
2-4 TABLESPOONS VEGETABLE OIL

Preheat oven to 250°F. In a large mixing bowl, mix all ingredients except oil.

In a large skillet, heat oil. Drop heaping tablespoons of mixture into skillet; flatten slightly. Cook about 5 minutes until golden brown on both sides. Keep cakes warm on a towel-lined baking sheet in the oven.

PREPARATION TIME: 25 MINUTES
COOKING TIME: 20 MINUTES
MAKES: 24

Borrowing from the inventive French cook again, we discover the quiche or custard pie as a natural for a summer squash dish. The availability of frozen pie shells makes this classic dish a cinch. For the diet-conscious, a crustless quiche is recommended.

ZUCCHINI-CRUMB QUICHE

1	CUP DRY BREAD CRUMBS
1	MEDIUM ZUCCHINI
2	TABLESPOONS OLIVE OIL
¼	CUP MARGARINE
¼	CUP ALL-PURPOSE FLOUR
⅔	CUP SCALDED MILK
½	CUP GRATED ROMANO CHEESE
1	EGG, BEATEN
¼	TEASPOON GROUND NUTMEG
¼	TEASPOON SALT
⅛	TEASPOON FRESHLY GROUND BLACK PEPPER

Preheat oven to 350° F. Butter a 9-inch pie pan and line with bread crumbs.

Cut zucchini into very thin slices. Allow to drain on paper towels. In a small skillet, sauté zucchini in olive oil. Drain again on paper towels.

In a large saucepan, melt margarine. Add flour and milk, stirring until thick. Stir in cheese, egg, and seasonings. Add zucchini and ladle into prepared pie pan. Bake for 35 minutes.

PREPARATION TIME: 15 MINUTES
BAKING TIME: 35 MINUTES
SERVES: 4

ZUCCHINI QUICHE

2	CUPS THINLY SLICED ZUCCHINI
1	CUP SLICED ONIONS
1	CLOVE GARLIC, MINCED
3	TABLESPOONS OLIVE OIL
1½	TEASPOONS SALT
1	10-INCH PIE SHELL, UNBAKED
4	EGGS, BEATEN
1	CUP MILK
1	CUP HEAVY CREAM
½	CUP GRATED LOW-FAT MOZZARELLA CHEESE

Preheat oven to 375°F. In a large skillet, sauté zucchini, onions, and garlic in olive oil. Season with salt. Cover bottom of pie shell with this mixture.

Combine remaining ingredients and pour into pie shell. Bake 30-35 minutes, or until quiche is set. Serve hot or cold.

PREPARATION TIME: 10 MINUTES
BAKING TIME: 30-35 MINUTES
SERVES: 6

SAUCE QUICHE ITALIANO

2 CUPS THINLY SLICED ZUCCHINI
   OR OTHER SUMMER SQUASH
1 CUP THINLY SLICED ONIONS
1 CLOVE GARLIC, MINCED
3 TABLESPOONS OLIVE OIL
2 TEASPOONS SALT
2 MEDIUM TOMATOES, PEELED
   AND CHOPPED
1 CUP TOMATO SAUCE
¼ TEASPOON DRIED OREGANO
¼ TEASPOON DRIED TARRAGON
2 CUPS SMALL CURD COTTAGE
   CHEESE
3 EGGS
¾ CUP MILK
½ CUP GRATED LOW-FAT
   MOZZARELLA CHEESE
1 10-INCH PIE SHELL, UNBAKED

Preheat oven to 350°F. In a large skillet, sauté zucchini, onions, and garlic in oil. Season with salt. Remove and set aside.

Simmer tomatoes, tomato sauce, and remaining seasonings until tomatoes are soft. Set aside. Mix well cottage cheese, eggs, and milk in a medium mixing bowl.

Place zucchini mixture in the pie shell. Add egg mixture and 4 tablespoons of tomato mixture. Bake 35 minutes.

Sprinkle on mozzarella cheese and return to oven until cheese melts. Serve quiche with remaining tomato mixture.

PREPARATION TIME: 20 MINUTES
BAKING TIME: 35 MINUTES
SERVES: 6

ZUCCHINI-SALMON QUICHE

1⅔ CUPS SHREDDED ZUCCHINI
¼ CUP CHOPPED ONIONS
    WATER
3 EGGS, BEATEN
½ CUP GRATED PARMESAN
    CHEESE
1 TABLESPOON LEMON JUICE
¼ CUP CHOPPED FRESH PARSLEY
¼ TEASPOON SALT
¼ TEASPOON DRIED DILL WEED
    PEPPER TO TASTE
1 8-OUNCE CAN SALMON, DRAINED
    AND FLAKED

Preheat oven to 325° F. Combine zucchini and onions in a large saucepan with water to cover. Bring to a boil, reduce heat, and simmer, covered, until tender. Drain mixture, pressing out liquid.

In a medium mixing bowl, combine remaining ingredients, mix well, add to zucchini mixture, and pour into an ungreased 9-inch pie pan. Bake for 25-30 minutes, or until pie has set.

PREPARATION TIME: 10 MINUTES
BAKING TIME: 25-30 MINUTES
SERVES: 8

SOUFFLÉS

The French verb *souffler* means "to blow," and the thought of attempting a soufflé is enough to blow the mind of some cooks. This is unfortunate, for a delicious soufflé is not that difficult to prepare. Granted, there are some pitfalls to avoid, but this is true with many dishes.

A good recipe, steady heat, and a well-prepared soufflé dish are the only requirements. The soufflé dish should be well-greased and floured and of an appropriate size. The height of a soufflé dish may be extended by encircling it with a strip of wax paper. A long double thickness of the paper tied around the dish so that it extends two inches above the rim will give your soufflé the chance to puff up or "blow up" beautifully without fear of its overflowing the limits of the container.

Pumpkin and winter squash are interchangeable in these recipes.

ZUCCHINI SOUFFLÉ

3 MEDIUM ZUCCHINI
  SALT
½ CUP WATER
1 TABLESPOON MARGARINE
1 TABLESPOON ALL-PURPOSE
  FLOUR
½ CUP SCALDED MILK
1 TEASPOON LEMON JUICE
⅓ CUP GRATED GRUYÈRE CHEESE
2 EGG YOLKS, BEATEN
4 EGG WHITES
  WATER

Preheat oven to 350°F. Cut zucchini into very thin slices crosswise. Spread on paper towels. Sprinkle with salt and allow to drain for 1 hour. Rinse and drain dry. Place zucchini in a small saucepan with water. Simmer until transparent. Drain.

In a small saucepan, melt margarine and add flour, stirring until smooth. Slowly pour in milk and stir until sauce thickens.

In a large mixing bowl, combine zucchini, white sauce, lemon juice, and cheese with egg yolks. Beat egg whites until stiff. Gently fold egg whites into zucchini mixture.

Pour into a well-greased and floured 4-cup soufflé dish. Place soufflé in a pan of water and bake for 45 minutes.

> PREPARATION TIME: 1 HOUR 20 MINUTES
> BAKING TIME: 45 MINUTES
> SERVES: 2

SQUASH SOUFFLÉ

4 CUPS WINTER SQUASH PULP
4 TABLESPOONS MARGARINE
½ TEASPOON SALT
3 TABLESPOONS BROWN SUGAR
¼ TEASPOON GROUND NUTMEG
1 TABLESPOON GRATED ORANGE
    OR LEMON PEEL
    PEPPER TO TASTE
5 EGG YOLKS, BEATEN
5 EGG WHITES

Preheat oven to 350°F. Squash may be baked whole in oven for about an hour. Puncture rind to let steam escape. When cooked, cut open squash and remove seeds and stringy portion. Mash pulp and combine with the next seven ingredients in a large mixing bowl.

Beat egg whites until stiff. Fold egg whites into squash mixture. Pour into a well-greased and floured 6-cup soufflé dish. Bake 40 minutes. May be served with a sauce of orange marmalade and pineapple juice heated or maple syrup and lemon juice.

PREPARATION TIME: 1 HOUR 15 MINUTES
BAKING TIME: 40 MINUTES
SERVES: 6

SQUASH AND CORN SOUFFLÉ

3 MEDIUM SUMMER SQUASH,
   UNPEELED
2¼ TEASPOONS SALT
6 TABLESPOONS BUTTER
3 GREEN ONIONS, CHOPPED
2 EARS FRESH CORN
   WATER
6 TABLESPOONS ALL-PURPOSE
   FLOUR
¼ TEASPOON SALT
¼ TEASPOON FRESHLY GROUND
   BLACK PEPPER
1¼ CUPS MILK
6 EGGS, SEPARATED
½ CUP GRATED SWISS CHEESE

Preheat oven to 350°F. Coarsely grate unpeeled squash and sprinkle with 1 teaspoon salt. Place in a sieve and drain for 5 minutes. Press out remaining moisture. In a medium skillet, sauté squash in 1 tablespoon butter for 5 minutes. Add onions.

Simmer corn in boiling water for 5 minutes. Drain and cut kernels from cob.

In a small saucepan, heat remaining butter, blend in flour, salt, and pepper, and mix well. Bring mixture to a slow boil, reduce heat, and gradually add milk. Cook until mixture thickens.

In a large mixing bowl, beat egg yolks and gradually add milk mixture, stirring constantly. Mix in cheese, squash, and corn.

Beat egg whites until stiff and gradually mix into yolk mixture. Pour into a well-greased and floured 8-cup soufflé dish. Bake until golden on top, about 55 minutes.

PREPARATION TIME: 25 MINUTES
BAKING TIME: 55 MINUTES
SERVES: 6

SOUPS

Unless we eat at a rather expensive restaurant, few of us dine in such elaborate circumstances as to regard soup as a first course. Informal and economical dining has promoted soup to main course status at both noon and evening meals. "Chewy" or thick soups, not far removed from the stew category, make hearty meals in themselves, usually complemented by French, Italian, or a hearty wholegrain bread. Lighter, more delicate soups, of either a cream or clear variety, served with salad, sandwiches, crackers, or whatever may be an appropriate and filling accompaniment, make appetizing luncheon and supper fare.

Homemade vegetable soup will never be outdone by the canned varieties. The cook who prepares soup from scratch knows how wise it is to have frozen vegetables, packaged together or in small separate portions for later combining, to plop in the soup at a moment's notice. In other chapters, suggested vegetable combinations and packaging for freezing can help you prepare ahead for soups and stews, full of tender and nutritious vegetables to be enjoyed long after the gardening season is over.

This first soup may be served either hot or cold just as you might in the case of Vichyssoise, which is made with potatoes and appears with expected frequency on the dinner menus of most fine restaurants. Squashyssoise may be made of zucchini, crookneck, straightneck, or a combination of all three.

SQUASHYSSOISE (SQUASH SOUP)

4 **MEDIUM ONIONS, MINCED**
2 **TABLESPOONS MARGARINE**
2 **CUPS SLICED SUMMER SQUASH**
4 **CUPS CHICKEN BROTH OR**
   BOUILLON
1 **CUP MILK OR CREAM**
   SALT AND PEPPER TO TASTE

In a medium skillet, sauté onions in margarine until translucent. Remove onions and set aside. Sauté squash until soft. Add 1 cup chicken broth.

Pour this mixture gradually with the reserved onions into a blender or food processor. Return to a large saucepan along with remaining broth, milk, and seasonings. Serve hot or cold.

PREPARATION TIME: 15 MINUTES
COOKING TIME: 10 MINUTES
SERVES: 4

WINTER SQUASH AND SHRIMP BISQUE

5 **CUPS ACORN, BUTTERNUT,**
   SWEET MAMA SQUASH, CUBED
   AND PEELED
½ **CUP BUTTER**
1 **CUP DICED ONIONS**
½ **CUP ALL-PURPOSE FLOUR**
5 **CUPS CHICKEN BROTH**
1 **CUP DRY WHITE WINE**
1 **CUP HALF-AND-HALF**
   SALT AND PEPPER TO TASTE
1 **POUND SHRIMP, UNCOOKED**

Microwave punctured winter squash on HIGH for 6-8 minutes, or bake conventionally until almost tender.

In a large saucepan, melt butter, add onions, and cook until soft. Add flour and stir over heat for 3 minutes. Add broth and bring to a boil while stirring. Add squash pulp, wine, and simmer for several minutes.

Stir in half-and-half and season. Puree mixture in a blender or food processor.

Return soup to the saucepan, add shrimp, and heat thoroughly until shrimp are cooked, 3-5 minutes. Serve hot.

PREPARATION TIME: 20 MINUTES
COOKING TIME: 15 MINUTES
SERVES: 6

ZUCCHINI-SPAGHETTI SOUP

1   MEDIUM ONION, MINCED
1   CLOVE GARLIC, MINCED
¼   CUP OLIVE OIL
5   CUPS THINLY SLICED
      ZUCCHINI
1   MEDIUM TOMATO, PEELED AND
      CHOPPED
½   TEASPOON DRIED BASIL
      SALT AND PEPPER TO TASTE
1   CUP VEGETABLE STOCK OR
      CHICKEN BROTH
½   POUND UNCOOKED SPAGHETTI
      OR 4 CUPS SPAGHETTI
      SQUASH FIBERS

Sauté onion and garlic in olive oil in a large saucepan. Add zucchini rounds, tomato, seasonings, and stock. Cover and simmer over low heat 1½ hours.

Add short lengths of uncooked spaghetti and continue simmering another 10 minutes. *Note:* If vegetable stock and spaghetti squash are used, this is an all-vegetable dish!

PREPARATION TIME: 10 MINUTES
COOKING TIME: 1 HOUR 40 MINUTES
SERVE: 4

CREAM OF SQUASH SOUP

1   CUP MINCED ONIONS
2   TABLESPOONS MARGARINE
2 ½   CUPS CHICKEN BROTH
1   CUP COOKED WINTER SQUASH
½   TEASPOON GROUND CINNAMON
¼   TEASPOON GROUND NUTMEG
      SALT AND PEPPER TO TASTE
¾   CUP CREAM OR MILK
      CROUTONS, TOASTED

In a large saucepan, sauté onions in margarine until tender. Add 1 cup chicken broth and simmer 10 minutes. Gradually pour into a blender or food processor and blend thoroughly. Return to the saucepan.

Add squash, remaining broth, and seasonings. Bring to a boil. Reduce heat and stir until smooth. Cover and simmer 10 minutes.

Add cream. If milk is used, add an additional 2 tablespoons of margarine. Serve with toasted croutons.

PREPARATION TIME: 15 MINUTES
COOKING TIME: 25 MINUTES
SERVES: 4

SQUASH-BEAN SOUP

1   **POUND DRY NAVY BEANS**
8   **CUPS WATER**
6   **CUPS WINTER SQUASH, COOKED**
    OR 6 CUPS SUMMER SQUASH,
      PEELED AND CUBED
1   **HAM BONE WITH SOME MEAT**
1   **CUP CHOPPED ONIONS**
1   **CUP CHOPPED CELERY**
1   **CUP CHOPPED CARROTS**
    SALT AND PEPPER TO TASTE

In a large cooking pot, soak beans in water to cover overnight or according to directions on package. Do **not** drain.

Add *cooked* winter squash or *uncooked* summer squash. Add ham bone, onions, celery, carrots, and seasonings. Bring mixture to a boil. Cover, reduce heat, and simmer for 1 hour.

Remove bone and set aside. Put at least half of mixture in a blender or food processor and puree. Return to the cooking pot. Cut meat from bone, dice, and add to soup mixture. Add additional water for desired consistency.

Simmer soup, covered for an additional 20 minutes. Check seasonings.

> *PREPARATION TIME: 25 MINUTES*
> *COOKING TIME: 1 HOUR 20 MINUTES*
> *SERVES: 8*

CURRIED SQUASH SOUP

6   **SMALL SUMMER SQUASH, CUT**
      INTO SMALL PIECES
1   **LARGE ONION, THINLY SLICED**
1   **TEASPOON CURRY POWDER**
½   **TEASPOON DRY MUSTARD**
3   **CUPS CHICKEN BROTH**
3   **TABLESPOONS UNCOOKED RICE**
1½ **CUPS MILK**
    SALT AND PEPPER TO TASTE
    FRESH CHIVES, CHOPPED
      (OPTIONAL)

In a large saucepan, combine squash, onion, curry powder, mustard, broth, and rice. Bring mixture to a boil, reduce heat, and simmer, covered, for 40 minutes.

Pour mixture into a blender or food processor. Add milk and seasonings and puree. Chill for at least 2 hours. May also be served hot by reheating but not allowing to boil. Chives may be used as garnish.

> *PREPARATION TIME: 2 HOURS 20 MINUTES*
> *COOKING TIME: 40 MINUTES*
> *SERVES: 6*

WINTER SQUASH AND APPLE SOUP

1   MEDIUM BUTTERNUT SQUASH,
    CUT INTO PIECES
4   TART GREEN APPLES, PEELED,
    CORED, AND CHOPPED
4   CUPS CHICKEN BROTH
1   CUP FRESH BREAD CRUMBS
1   MEDIUM ONION, CHOPPED
½   TEASPOON DRIED ROSEMARY
½   TEASPOON DRIED MARJORAM
    SALT AND PEPPER TO TASTE
    FRESH PARSLEY, MINCED

Parboil pieces of squash and peel. Combine all ingredients except parsley in a large saucepan and bring to a boil. Simmer until tender.

Puree batches of mixture in a blender or food processor. Check seasonings. Cover and refrigerate. Can be frozen in batches and thawed overnight. Garnish with fresh parsley and serve hot.

PREPARATION TIME: 20 MINUTES
COOKING TIME: 20 MINUTES
SERVES: 12

SUMMER SQUASH AND BLOSSOM SOUP

4   SHALLOTS
4   TABLESPOONS UNSALTED
     BUTTER
10   CUPS YELLOW SQUASH
3   QUARTS CHICKEN BROTH
     SALT AND PEPPER TO TASTE
8-12 SQUASH BLOSSOMS

In a large skillet, mince shallots and sauté in butter for 10 minutes. Chop squash, add to shallots, and sauté for 5 minutes. Add broth to cover squash and cook until tender, about 10 minutes.

Cool mixture and puree in a blender or food processor. Season and add more hot broth if mixture is too thick. Cut squash blossom petals into fine strips. Serve soup in warm bowls and garnish with blossom strips.

PREPARATION TIME: 15 MINUTES
COOKING TIME: 25 MINUTES
SERVES: 8

SQUASH BLOSSOM SOUP

3 TABLESPOONS BUTTER
1 SMALL ONION, CHOPPED
1 CLOVE GARLIC, MINCED
3 DOZEN SQUASH OR PUMPKIN
    BLOSSOMS, CHOPPED
3 CUPS CHICKEN BROTH
1 CUP HALF-AND-HALF
    SALT AND PEPPER TO TASTE

In a large saucepan, melt butter. Add onion and garlic and cook until soft. Add blossoms and stir until softened. Add broth and bring to a boil. Reduce heat and simmer for 10 minutes.

Pour mixture into a blender or food processor and blend until pureed. Return mixture to the saucepan, slowly add half-and-half, and season to taste.

PREPARATION TIME: 15 MINUTES
COOKING TIME: 10 MINUTES
SERVES: 4

SOUP IN A PUMPKIN

1 WELL-SHAPED 5-POUND
    PUMPKIN
1 CUP GRATED CHEESE
    (MOZZARELLA OR GRUYÈRE)
1 CUP COOKED CHOPPED HAM
2 CUPS TOASTED CROUTONS
2 CUPS CREAM
    PINCH GROUND NUTMEG
    SALT AND PEPPER TO TASTE

Preheat oven to 325°F. Remove top of pumpkin. Scoop out seeds and stringy portion. Fill pumpkin with layers of cheese, ham, and croutons.

In a small mixing bowl, combine cream and seasonings. Pour into pumpkin, adding more cream if necessary to fill shell. Cover with aluminum foil and place pumpkin in a large baking pan. Bake 1½-2 hours, stirring several times.

Remove pumpkin from oven. Place on large serving dish. Top with pumpkin lid and serve soup from pumpkin "bowl."

PREPARATION TIME: 25 MINUTES
BAKING TIME: 1½-2 HOURS
SERVES: 4

STEWS

A stew is a stew, whether it's called a ragout, pot-au-feu, burgoo, goulash, omido, or estofado. The basic principle underlying stew preparation is a successful combination of meat, broth, vegetables, and seasonings.

Zucchini and other summer squash are natural partners with meat and other vegetables. The delicate flavors of green and yellow summer squash join tomatoes, onions, carrots, corn, potatoes, peas, celery, turnips, cauliflower, and beans to produce a delicious vegetarian stew. Veal, pork, beef, chicken, and turkey are all complemented by summer squash. Winter varieties make substantial and tasty contributions to stews and casseroles as well, as you will discover in the recipes which follow. Some of these have been adapted from foreign dishes indigenous to areas and countries in which squash has long been standard fare. Courgettes, marrows, cocozelles, and especially zucchini have been around for a long time in other parts of the world. Isn't it fortunate that gardeners are finally realizing the possibilities these prolific vegetables provide.

ZUCCHINI-SHORT RIB STEW

2 **POUNDS SHORT RIBS**
2 **TABLESPOONS VEGETABLE OIL**
1 **CUP WATER**
  SALT AND PEPPER TO TASTE
  VEGETABLE OIL
1 **LARGE ONION, CHOPPED**
2 **CUPS SLICED ZUCCHINI**
1 **9-OUNCE CAN CRUSHED PINEAPPLE**
1 **CUP PEELED AND CHOPPED TOMATOES**
1 **8-OUNCE PACKAGE EGG NOODLES, COOKED**

In a large saucepan, brown meat in oil. Add water, salt, and pepper. Cover and simmer 2 hours. Skim fat. Remove meat and set aside. Add enough water to remaining broth to make 1 cup and set aside.

In the pan with additional oil, sauté onion and zucchini until soft. Including reserved broth, mix in all ingredients except noodles and simmer gently about 20 minutes. Serve over hot noodles.

PREPARATION TIME: 15 MINUTES
COOKING TIME: 2 HOURS 20 MINUTES
SERVES: 4

GRILLED ZUCCHINI STEW IN FOIL

2 POUNDS STEW BEEF, CUBED
2 MEDIUM ZUCCHINI, SLICED
4 MEDIUM POTATOES, PEELED
  AND CUBED
2 SMALL ONIONS, SLICED
4 CARROTS, SLICED ¼ INCH
  THICK
2 CANS CONDENSED CREAM OF
  MUSHROOM SOUP, UNDILUTED
SALT AND PEPPER TO TASTE

Combine all ingredients in a large mixing bowl and mix well. Prepare six 18-inch squares of heavy-duty aluminum foil. Divide stew into six equal portions and spoon into foil. Season well. Join four corners of each square and twist top of bundles to seal. Refrigerate until fire is suitable for cooking.

An even fire of hot gray coals is preferable to a red hot one. Grill for 50-60 minutes, never allowing fire to flame. This is a great camping dish since stew may be served in foil packages, and there are no dishes to wash. *Note:* This stew may be made without meat. Simply increase amount of vegetables.

PREPARATION TIME: 15 MINUTES
COOKING TIME: 50-60 MINUTES
SERVES: 4

WINTER SQUASH-BEEF STEW

3 POUNDS STEW BEEF, CUT INTO
  1-INCH CUBES
  ALL-PURPOSE FLOUR
2 TABLESPOONS VEGETABLE OIL
4 MEDIUM ONIONS, SLICED
2½ CUPS WATER
½ TEASPOON DRIED THYME
½ TEASPOON DRIED BASIL
3 MEDIUM POTATOES, PEELED
  AND CUBED
2½ CUPS SLICED CARROTS
1½ CUPS PEAS
2 CUPS WINTER SQUASH, CUT
  INTO BITE-SIZED CHUNKS
3 OUNCES TOMATO PASTE

Dredge meat in flour. Heat oil in a Dutch oven. Brown meat and sauté onions. Add water and seasonings. Reduce heat and simmer 50 minutes.

Add potatoes, carrots, and peas. Cook 15 minutes more. Add squash and tomato paste and continue cooking for an additional 10 minutes until vegetables are tender.

PREPARATION TIME: 15 MINUTES
COOKING TIME: 1 HOUR 15 MINUTES
SERVES: 6

RAGOUT OF SUMMER SQUASH

6 CUPS SLICED SUMMER SQUASH
2 TABLESPOONS OLIVE OIL
2 TABLESPOONS MELTED
   MARGARINE
3 LARGE ONIONS, SLICED
2 LARGE GREEN PEPPERS,
   CHOPPED
2 CELERY STALKS, DICED
2 MEDIUM TOMATOES, PEELED
   AND QUARTERED
1 TABLESPOON CHOPPED FRESH
   PARSLEY
1 TABLESPOON EACH DRIED
   BASIL AND DRIED TARRAGON
1 CLOVE GARLIC
   SALT AND PEPPER TO TASTE
   PARMESAN CHEESE, GRATED

In a large saucepan, sauté squash on both sides in oil and melted margarine until soft. Remove and set aside.

Sauté onions, peppers, and celery. Add tomatoes and seasonings. Cook gently 30 minutes. Add reserved squash the last 5 minutes. Sprinkle with cheese.

> *PREPARATION TIME: 20 MINUTES*
> *COOKING TIME: 30 MINUTES*
> *SERVES: 4-6*

STEW IN A PUMPKIN

1 WELL-SHAPED 5-6-POUND
  PUMPKIN
  SALT AND PEPPER TO TASTE
  WATER
  MARGARINE
2 POUNDS STEW BEEF, CUT INTO
  1-INCH CUBES
¼ CUP ALL-PURPOSE FLOUR
2 TABLESPOONS VEGETABLE OIL
2 CLOVES GARLIC, MINCED
1 LARGE ONION, SLICED
1 CUP RED WINE
2 CUPS BEEF BROTH
½ TEASPOON SALT
½ TEASPOON DRIED THYME
1 BAY LEAF
1 CUP PEELED AND CHOPPED
  TOMATOES
2 MEDIUM ZUCCHINI, SLICED
1 20-OUNCE CAN GARBANZO
  BEANS, DRAINED
2 CARROTS, SLICED
2 MEDIUM POTATOES, PEELED
  AND CUBED

Preheat oven to 350°F. Remove lid of pumpkin and retain for later use. Scoop out seeds and stringy portion. Score inside several times. Rub interior surface with salt and pepper. Place pumpkin upside down in a large shallow pan, place lid in pan beside pumpkin. Add ¼-inch water and bake for 1 hour, or until tender.

Remove pumpkin from oven. Drain water and return upright pumpkin to the baking pan. Rub inside surfaces with margarine.

Dredge meat in flour. In a large skillet, brown meat in oil with garlic. Add onions and simmer until soft. Stir in wine, broth, and seasonings and cook over low heat until meat is tender, about 1 hour.

Add all vegetables and simmer 45 minutes. Spoon stew into warm pumpkin. The pumpkin pulp may be eaten with the stew.

PREPARATION TIME: 20 MINUTES
COOKING TIME: 1 HOUR 45 MINUTES
SERVES: 4

CHAPTER 11
PICKLES & RELISHES

Pickling need not be limited to cucumbers, especially since cucumbers are tricky to grow and the pickling variety difficult to find in the markets. A lot of people who enjoy pickles and the process of pickling them ought to try putting the good old zucchini in a jar which contains a delicious pickling solution.

Served with cold sandwiches or hamburgers, or added to an antipasto, the versatile zucchini lends itself to several tasty pickling preparations.

ZUCCHINI XMAS PICKLES FROM THE GARDEN

2 MEDIUM RED BELL PEPPERS
5 OR 6 SMALL ZUCCHINI
20 GREEN CHERRY TOMATOES
4 HEADS FRESH DILL *OR* 4
    TEASPOONS DRIED DILL SEED
4 CLOVES GARLIC
4 WHOLE CLOVES
3 CUPS WATER
1 CUP WHITE VINEGAR
2 TABLESPOONS SALT

Seed peppers and cut into rings. Cut zucchini into sticks to stand in pint glass jars. Pack all vegetables into hot sterilized glass pint jars allowing ½ inch headspace. In each jar, add head of fresh dill or dill seed, garlic clove, and a whole clove.

In a large saucepan, bring water, vinegar, and salt to a boil. Pour over vegetables in the jars. Seal with canning lids and process in boiling water bath for 20 minutes.

PREPARATION TIME: 20 MINUTES
COOKING TIME: 20 MINUTES
MAKES: 4 PINTS

RAINBOW PICKLES

8 CUPS SEVERAL TYPES OF
    GREEN AND YELLOW SUMMER
    SQUASH, CUT INTO SPEARS
2 MEDIUM ONIONS, CUT INTO
    RINGS
1 MEDIUM RED BELL PEPPER, CUT
    INTO STRIPS
    ICE
¼ CUP PICKLING SALT
2½ CUPS WHITE VINEGAR
1½ CUPS SUGAR
1 TABLESPOON MIXED PICKLING
    SPICES
2 TEASPOONS MUSTARD SEEDS
    FRESH DILL *OR* 2 TABLESPOONS
    DRIED DILL SEED

Combine vegetables in a large shallow pan, add ice, and allow mixture to chill for 15 minutes. Drain.

In a large saucepan, combine remaining ingredients and bring to a boil. Remove from heat and pour over vegetables. Refrigerate several days before using. Pack surplus in hot sterilized pint glass jars and keep refrigerated to be used in two weeks, or process in hot water bath for 10 minutes.

PREPARATION TIME: 25 MINUTES
MAKES: 4 PINTS

PUMPKIN PICKLES

8 CUPS PEELED AND CUBED
    PUMPKIN
2½ CUPS WHITE VINEGAR
2½ CUPS SUGAR
4 STICKS CINNAMON
1 TEASPOON PICKLING SPICES
1 TEASPOON GROUND CLOVES

Blanch bite-sized cubes over, *not in*, boiling water until tender. Combine remaining ingredients and bring to a rolling boil. Reduce heat and simmer 10 minutes.

Add pumpkin cubes and simmer an additional 5 minutes. Pack into hot sterilized pint glass jars. Seal and process in a boiling water bath for 5 minutes.

> *PREPARATION TIME: 30 MINUTES*
> *COOKING TIME: 25 MINUTES*
> *MAKES: 4 PINTS*

BRINED SQUASH PICKLES

1½ CUPS PICKLING SALT
    WATER
9½ POUNDS SMALL ZUCCHINI, CUT
    INTO 3- OR 4-INCH SPEARS OR
    A MIXTURE OF SQUASH AND
    CUCUMBERS
6 POUNDS CAULIFLOWER, BROKEN
    INTO FLORETS
12 CUPS WATER
12 CUPS SUGAR
8 CUPS WHITE VINEGAR
8 STICKS CINNAMON

Dissolve salt in boiling water to cover and pour into a large mixing bowl containing prepared vegetables. Cool and cover with weighted plate to keep vegetables in the brine. Let mixture stand in a cool place *for a week*. Temperature should not exceed 70°F. Sixty degrees is ideal.

Drain and discard brine. Cover vegetables with hot water to cover and let stand for *24 hours*. Drain.

Combine remaining ingredients in a large kettle and bring to a boil. Pour mixture over vegetables.

Repeat the draining, reserving syrup and reheating it the next morning for *four consecutive days*. Allow the vegetables to cool before covering.

On the last day, bring vegetables and syrup to a boil and pack into hot sterilized pint glass jars, leaving ½-inch headspace. Process in a boiling water bath for 5 minutes.

> *PREPARATION TIME: 30 MINUTES*
> *COOKING TIME: 5 MINUTES*
> *MAKES: 6 PINTS*

HOT DOG RELISH

9 CUPS CHOPPED ZUCCHINI
2 MEDIUM GREEN TOMATOES,
  CHOPPED
2 MEDIUM APPLES, CHOPPED
4 SMALL ONIONS, PEELED
4½ TEASPOONS SALT
1½ TEASPOONS FRESHLY
   GROUND BLACK PEPPER
1½ TEASPOONS GROUND CINNAMON
¾ TEASPOON GROUND CLOVES
2 CUPS SUGAR
1 PINT WHITE VINEGAR

Prepare vegetables and apples and set aside.

Combine remaining ingredients and bring to a boil in a large kettle. Add vegetables and fruit and simmer uncovered until thick, about 30 minutes. Stir frequently.

Pack into hot sterilized pint glass jars and process in a boiling water bath for 20 minutes.

> *PREPARATION TIME: 20 MINUTES*
> *COOKING TIME: 50 MINUTES*
> *MAKES: 4 PINTS*

RATATOUILLE RELISH

2 MEDIUM ZUCCHINI
2 MEDIUM GREEN PEPPERS
2 MEDIUM TOMATOES
1 SMALL EGGPLANT, PARED
2 TABLESPOONS SALT
1 CUP SUGAR
1 CUP WHITE VINEGAR
1 TEASPOON MUSTARD SEED
¾ TEASPOON CELERY SEED

Chop vegetables coarsely. Stir in salt and let stand for *12 hours*. Rinse and drain.

Combine remaining ingredients in a large saucepan. Add vegetables, mix well, and bring to a boil. Reduce heat and simmer 5 minutes, stirring frequently.

Cover and chill until served.

> *PREPARATION TIME: 20 MINUTES*
> *COOKING TIME: 10 MINUTES*
> *MAKES: ABOUT 4 CUPS*

ITALIAN RELISH

½ CUP CHOPPED ONIONS
1 CLOVE GARLIC, MINCED
2 TABLESPOONS OLIVE OIL
2 MEDIUM SUMMER SQUASH, CHOPPED
1 8-OUNCE CAN STEWED TOMATOES
1 8-OUNCE CAN PIZZA SAUCE
¼ TEASPOON DRIED OREGANO
¼ TEASPOON DRIED ROSEMARY
¼ TEASPOON DRIED THYME
SALT AND PEPPER TO TASTE

In a large skillet, sauté onions and garlic in olive oil until tender. Stir in squash, stewed tomatoes and liquid, pizza sauce, and seasonings. Bring to a boil, reduce heat, cover, and simmer for 10-12 minutes.

Uncover and continue cooking until relish is of preferred consistency. Serve hot or cold over meat or chicken.

> PREPARATION TIME: 15 MINUTES
> COOKING TIME: 20 MINUTES
> MAKES: 2½ CUPS

GRAND SCALE ZUCCHINI RELISH

10 CUPS MINCED ZUCCHINI
1 CUP PICKLING SALT
5 CUPS MINCED ONIONS
1 CUP DICED CELERY
3 MEDIUM GREEN PEPPERS, DICED
2 MEDIUM RED BELL PEPPERS, DICED
2 TEASPOONS TURMERIC
1 TABLESPOON DRY MUSTARD
3 TABLESPOONS CELERY SEED
6 CUPS SUGAR
5 CUPS WHITE VINEGAR
3 TABLESPOONS CORNSTARCH

Prepare zucchini. Combine with salt and other vegetables in a large shallow pan. Allow mixture to stand overnight.

Drain. Rinse thoroughly and drain again in a colander. Press a bowl down on top of vegetable mixture to force out as much liquid as possible.

In a large enamel pot, combine remaining ingredients. Add vegetables and bring to a rolling boil. Reduce heat and boil gently 20 minutes. Ladle relish into hot sterilized pint glass jars and seal.

> PREPARATION TIME: 55 MINUTES
> COOKING TIME: 20 MINUTES
> MAKES: 8 PINTS

CHAPTER 12

BREADS
& BUTTER

Accustomed as we are to uninspiring commercially processed bread, we are likely to have become complacent about tasteless and virtually nutritionless bread.

Breadmaking is, admittedly, a time-consuming activity and many cooks are not interested enough to undertake such a project. Others have made noble breadmaking attempts only to fail because of inadequate recipes, poor equipment, yeast failure, or inadvertent mistakes. How demoralizing to acquire all the proper ingredients, combine them, knead the dough interminably, impatiently survive the rising, bake the bread, and yet at serving time, discover the whole aromatic mess won't even yield to a carving knife!

Have no fear. The squash bread recipes included here are virtually foolproof, and the results are so delicious you will receive all sorts of accolades. Serve any one of these great breads with one of your favorite squash soups or stews and you will please everyone who sits at your table—and sneak in extra nutrition, too.

NOTE: Oat bran flour may be substituted for about one-fourth of the flour specified in the bread recipes.

ZUCCHINI-CARROT CAKE

2   EGGS
1   CUP SUGAR
⅔   CUP VEGETABLE OIL
1¼ CUPS ALL-PURPOSE FLOUR
1   TEASPOON BAKING POWDER
1   TEASPOON BAKING SODA
1   TEASPOON GROUND CINNAMON
½   TEASPOON SALT
1   CUP GRATED CARROTS
1   CUP GRATED AND DRAINED
    ZUCCHINI
½   CUP CHOPPED NUTS

FROSTING:

1   3-OUNCE PACKAGE CREAM
    CHEESE, SOFTENED
3   TABLESPOONS MARGARINE
2   CUPS CONFECTIONERS' SUGAR
1   TEASPOON VANILLA EXTRACT

Preheat oven to 350°F. In a large mixing bowl, beat eggs with sugar until frothy. Gradually beat in oil. Add dry ingredients. Beat at high speed for 4 minutes.

Stir in carrots, zucchini, and nuts. Pour into a well-greased 9-inch square baking pan. Bake about 35 minutes, or until top springs back when lightly touched.

Frosting:

In a small mixing bowl, blend cream cheese and margarine. Add confectioners' sugar and vanilla. Beat until smooth. Spread evenly over cooled cake.

PREPARATION TIME: 30 MINUTES
BAKING TIME: 35 MINUTES
MAKES: 9-INCH SQUARE CAKE

PUMPKIN-APPLE TORTE

1   **CUP COOKED AND MASHED PUMPKIN**
3   **EGGS, BEATEN**
1   **CUP SUGAR**
¾   **CUP ALL-PURPOSE FLOUR**
1   **TEASPOON BAKING POWDER**
2   **TEASPOONS GROUND CINNAMON**
1   **TEASPOON GROUND GINGER**
½   **TEASPOON SALT**
½   **CUP PARED AND CHOPPED APPLE**
½   **CUP CHOPPED NUTS**
   WHIPPED TOPPING (OPTIONAL)

Preheat oven to 325°F. In a large mixing bowl, combine pumpkin with eggs and sugar. Stir in flour, baking powder, and seasonings. Stir in apples and nuts.

Pour batter into a well-greased, floured 8-inch round cake pan. Bake for 20-25 minutes, or until a tester inserted in the center comes out clean. May be served with whipped topping.

PREPARATION TIME: 15 MINUTES
BAKING TIME: 20-25 MINUTES
MAKES: 8-INCH ROUND CAKE

ZUCCHINI BREAD

3   **EGGS, BEATEN**
1   **CUP VEGETABLE OIL**
2½   **CUPS SUGAR**
2   **CUPS GRATED ZUCCHINI**
1   **TABLESPOON VANILLA EXTRACT**
¼   **TEASPOON BLACK WALNUT EXTRACT**
3   **CUPS ALL-PURPOSE FLOUR**
1   **TABLESPOON GROUND CINNAMON**
1   **TEASPOON SALT**
1   **TEASPOON BAKING SODA**
1¼   **TEASPOONS BAKING POWDER**
   RAISINS AND NUTS (OPTIONAL)

Preheat oven to 350°F. In a large mixing bowl, stir together eggs, oil, sugar, zucchini, and flavorings. Add dry ingredients and mix well.

Raisins and chopped nuts may be added if desired. Pour batter into two well-greased 8 x 4-inch loaf pans. Bake for 1 hour. Cool in the pans for 10 minutes.

PREPARATION TIME: 20 MINUTES
BAKING TIME: 1 HOUR
MAKES: 2 LOAVES

ZUCCHINI-BRAN BREAD

¾ CUP MELTED AND COOLED
    MARGARINE
¾ CUP EGG SUBSTITUTE
⅓ CUP SKIM MILK
¾ CUP BRAN CEREAL
½ CUP RAISINS
1¾ CUPS ALL-PURPOSE FLOUR
1 CUP SUGAR
2 TEASPOONS BAKING POWDER
1½ TEASPOONS GROUND CINNAMON
1 TEASPOON BAKING SODA
1½ CUPS GRATED ZUCCHINI, LIQUID
    PRESSED OUT

Preheat oven to 350°F. In a large mixing bowl, combine margarine, egg substitute, milk, cereal, and raisins. Let stand 5 minutes.

In a small mixing bowl, combine dry ingredients. Stir into cereal mixture. Add zucchini.

Spread batter into a well-greased 8 x 8 x 2-inch baking pan. Bake 55-60 minutes. Cool in the pan for 10 minutes.

> *PREPARATION TIME: 20 MINUTES*
> *BAKING TIME: 55-60 MINUTES*
> *MAKES: 18 PIECES*

ZUCCHINI LOAF

1 CUP COARSLY SHREDDED
    ZUCCHINI
⅔ CUP SUGAR
½ CUP SKIM MILK
¼ CUP VEGETABLE OIL
1¼ CUPS ALL-PURPOSE FLOUR
½ CUP OAT BRAN FLOUR
1 TEASPOON BAKING SODA
¼ TEASPOON BAKING POWDER
½ TEASPOON SALT
½ TEASPOON GROUND CINNAMON
1 TEASPOON VANILLA EXTRACT
VEGETABLE COOKING SPRAY

Preheat oven to 350°F. In a large bowl, combine first four ingredients. Combine next six ingredients. Stir into zucchini mixture until just moistened. Add vanilla extract.

Pour batter into an 8½ x 4½ x 3-inch loaf pan coated with cooking spray. Bake for 55 minutes, or until a tester inserted in the center comes out clean. Remove from pan and cool completely on a wire rack.

> *PREPARATION TIME: 25 MINUTES*
> *BAKING TIME: 55 MINUTES*
> *SERVES: 16*

ZUCCHINI-CARROT BREAD

3 EGGS
1 CUP VEGETABLE OIL
1½ CUPS PACKED BROWN SUGAR
1 CUP GRATED AND DRAINED
   ZUCCHINI
1 CUP GRATED CARROTS
2 TEASPOONS VANILLA EXTRACT
2½ CUPS ALL-PURPOSE FLOUR
1 TEASPOON BAKING SODA
1 TEASPOON BAKING POWDER
1 TEASPOON SALT
3 TEASPOONS GROUND CINNAMON
½ CUP BRAN CEREAL
1 CUP CHOPPED NUTS

Preheat oven to 350°F. In a large mixing bowl, beat eggs with oil. Stir in brown sugar, zucchini, carrots, and vanilla.

Sift in flour, baking soda, baking powder, salt, and cinnamon, and blend remaining ingredients into zucchini mixture, adding nuts last.

Pour batter into two well-greased 8 x 4-inch loaf pans. Bake 1 hour 30 minutes. Cool in the pans for 10 minutes.

PREPARATION TIME: 15 MINUTES
BAKING TIME: 1 HOUR 30 MINUTES
MAKES: 2 LOAVES

WINTER SQUASH BREAD

2 EGGS
¼ CUP MILK
1 CUP COOKED AND MASHED
   WINTER SQUASH
⅔ CUP VEGETABLE OIL
1 CUP PACKED BROWN SUGAR
½ CUP SORGHUM OR HONEY
2 CUPS ALL-PURPOSE FLOUR
1 TEASPOON BAKING SODA
½ TEASPOON BAKING POWDER
½ TEASPOON SALT
½ TEASPOON GROUND NUTMEG
½ TEASPOON GROUND CINNAMON
   RAISINS AND NUTS (OPTIONAL)

Preheat oven to 350°F. In a large mixing bowl, combine first six ingredients and mix well.

Sift in remaining ingredients. Beat at medium speed 2 minutes. Raisins and nuts may be added. Pour batter into a well-greased 9 x 5-inch loaf pan. Bake 1 hour 5 minutes. Cool in the pan for 10 minutes.

PREPARATION TIME: 15 MINUTES
BAKING TIME: 1 HOUR 5 MINUTES
MAKES: 1 LOAF

PUMPKIN NUT BREAD

⅓ CUP VEGETABLE OIL
1⅓ CUPS SUGAR
2 EGGS
1⅔ CUPS ALL-PURPOSE FLOUR
1 TEASPOON BAKING SODA
½ TEASPOON BAKING POWDER
½ TEASPOON SALT
½ TEASPOON PUMPKIN PIE SPICE
½ TEASPOON GROUND CINNAMON
1 CUP COOKED AND MASHED
     PUMPKIN
¼ CUP MILK
½ CUP CHOPPED NUTS

Preheat oven to 350°F. In a small mixing bowl, beat oil, sugar, and eggs at high speed for 3 minutes.

In a large mixing bowl, sift together dry ingredients, then stir in remaining ingredients. Beat until batter is smooth.

Pour batter into a well-greased 9 x 5-inch loaf pan. Bake for 1 hour. Cool in the pans for 10 minutes.

> PREPARATION TIME: 10 MINUTES
> BAKING TIME: 1 HOUR
> MAKES: 1 LOAF

PUMPKIN-APPLESAUCE TEA BREAD

2 CUPS SUGAR
⅓ CUP MOLASSES
1 CUP COOKED AND MASHED
     PUMPKIN
1 CUP APPLESAUCE
⅔ CUP VEGETABLE OIL
3 EGGS
⅓ CUP MILK
3⅔ CUPS ALL-PURPOSE FLOUR
1½ TEASPOONS BAKING POWDER
2 TEASPOONS BAKING SODA
2 TEASPOONS GROUND CINNAMON
1 TEASPOON GROUND NUTMEG
1 TEASPOON VANILLA EXTRACT
1 CUP CHOPPED NUTS
1 CUP RAISINS OR DATES

Preheat oven to 350°F. In a large mixing bowl, at medium speed, beat together first seven ingredients.

In another large mixing bowl, sift in dry ingredients, then add remaining ingredients and mix well.

Pour batter into two well-greased 9 x 5-inch loaf pans. Bake for 1 hour. Cool in the pans for 10 minutes. Wrap in aluminum foil and store overnight.

> PREPARATION TIME: 10 MINUTES
> BAKING TIME: 1 HOUR
> MAKES: 2 LOAVES

PUMPKIN RICE BREAD

2½ CUPS BROWN RICE FLOUR*
1 TABLESPOON BAKING POWDER
½ TEASPOON SALT
½ CUP MARGARINE
⅓ CUP MOLASSES
2 EGGS
2 CUPS COOKED AND MASHED
    PUMPKIN
½ CUP CHOPPED PECANS

Preheat oven to 325°F. Combine rice flour, baking powder, and salt in a small mixing bowl.

In a large mixing bowl, beat together margarine and molasses. Add eggs and beat mixture. Add pumpkin and continue beating. Slowly stir in dry ingredients and mix in pecans.

Pour batter into a well-greased 9 x 5-inch loaf pan. Bake for 45 minutes. Cover loaf with aluminum foil and continue baking for an additional 30 minutes.

Remove from oven and cool in the pan for 15 minutes. Remove loaf from the pan and cool on a wire rack.

*May purchase at health food store.

> PREPARATION TIME: 25 MINUTES
> BAKING TIME: 1 HOUR 15 MINUTES TOTAL
> MAKES: 1 LOAF

WHOLE-WHEAT ZUCCHINI MUFFINS

2 CUPS WHOLE-WHEAT FLOUR
3 TEASPOONS BAKING POWDER
1 TEASPOON GROUND CINNAMON
¼ TEASPOON SALT
2 EGGS
¾ CUP MILK
⅓ CUP VEGETABLE OIL
¼ CUP HONEY
1 CUP GRATED ZUCCHINI
⅔ CUP RAISINS

Preheat oven to 300°F. In a large mixing bowl, combine dry ingredients. Beat eggs, milk, oil, and honey in a separate large mixing bowl. Fold in dry ingredients, plus zucchini squash and raisins.

Stir gently and spoon into well-greased muffin tins. Bake until golden, about 20 minutes.

> PREPARATION TIME: 20 MINUTES
> BAKING TIME: 20 MINUTES
> MAKES: 12-15 MUFFINS

ZUCCHINI-BRAN BREAKFAST CAKE

1¼   CUPS BRAN CEREAL
1½   CUPS ALL-PURPOSE FLOUR
2   TEASPOONS BAKING POWDER
1   TEASPOON BAKING SODA
1   TEASPOON PUMPKIN PIE SPICE
1½   CUPS PACKED BROWN SUGAR
1   CUP MELTED MARGARINE
¾   CUP EGG SUBSTITUTE
2   TEASPOONS VANILLA EXTRACT
2   CUPS SHREDDED ZUCCHINI
1   CUP CHOPPED APPLES
     CONFECTIONERS' SUGAR
     (OPTIONAL)

Preheat oven to 350°F. In a large mixing bowl, combine cereal, flour, baking powder, baking soda, and pumpkin pie spice.

In a separate large mixing bowl, beat brown sugar, margarine, egg substitute, and vanilla until smooth. Stir in zucchini, apples, and cereal mixture.

Spread into a well-greased and floured 13 x 9 x 2-inch baking pan. Bake 40-45 minutes, or until a tester inserted in the center comes out clean. Cool 10 minutes.

Remove cake from pan. Cool on a wire rack. Sprinkle with confectioners' sugar if desired.

> *PREPARATION TIME: 20 MINUTES*
> *BAKING TIME: 40-45 MINUTES*
> *SERVES: 24*

ZUCCHINI-CHEDDAR BISCUITS

2   CUPS *UNPEELED* AND
     SHREDDED ZUCCHINI
1   TEASPOON SALT
3   CUPS ALL-PURPOSE FLOUR
1   TABLESPOON BAKING POWDER
2   TEASPOONS BAKING SODA
¼   TEASPOON FRESHLY GROUND
     BLACK PEPPER
3   TABLESPOONS COLD UNSALTED
     BUTTER
1   CUP SHREDDED CHEDDAR
     CHEESE
1   LARGE EGG
1½   CUPS BUTTERMILK

Preheat oven to 400°F. Place zucchini in a colander. Sprinkle with salt and let stand 30 minutes. Squeeze zucchini dry with hands and place in a small mixing bowl. Amount will be reduced to about a half cup.

Sift all dry ingredients together in a large mixing bowl. Cut in butter. Add cheese, egg, buttermilk, and reserved zucchini and toss with a fork to mix well. Place twenty-four spoonsful of batter onto a well-greased baking sheet. Bake 15 minutes.

> *PREPARATION TIME: 15 MINUTES*
> *BAKING TIME: 15 MINUTES*
> *MAKES: 24 BISCUITS*

ZUCCHINI-APPLE-CARROT MUFFINS

2 CUPS ALL-PURPOSE FLOUR
1 CUP SHREDDED ZUCCHINI
2 CUPS SHREDDED CARROTS
1¼ CUPS SUGAR
1 SWEET APPLE, CORED AND
  CHOPPED
¾ CUP GOLDEN RAISINS
¾ CUP SHREDDED UNSWEETENED
  COCONUT
½ CUP COARSELY CHOPPED
  PECANS
1 TABLESPOON GROUND
  CINNAMON
2 TEASPOONS BAKING SODA
1 TEASPOON VANILLA EXTRACT
½ TEASPOON SALT
3 EGGS
1 CUP VEGETABLE OIL

Preheat oven to 375°F. Combine everything except last two ingredients in a large mixing bowl. Beat eggs and oil separately in another large mixing bowl. Stir vegetable and apple mixture into egg mixture.

Spoon ¼ cup batter into each well-greased muffin tin. Bake 25 minutes, or until done.

PREPARATION TIME: 25 MINUTES
BAKING TIME: 25 MINUTES
MAKES: 24 MUFFINS

ZUCCHINI STUFFING

½ CUP CHOPPED CELERY
½ CUP CHOPPED ONIONS
3 TABLESPOONS MARGARINE
4 CUPS BREAD CUBES
4 CUPS CHOPPED ZUCCHINI OR
  OTHER SUMMER SQUASH
2 EGGS, SLIGHTLY BEATEN
½ CUP SHREDDED MILD CHEDDAR
  CHEESE
1 TEASPOON SALT
1 TEASPOON POULTRY SEASONING

In a large saucepan, cook celery and onions in margarine until tender. Remove from heat.

Add remaining ingredients and mix well.

PREPARATION TIME: 10 MINUTES
COOKING TIME: 5 MINUTES
MAKES: ENOUGH FOR A 10-POUND
  BIRD

BAKED PUMPKIN BUTTER

1 6-8-POUND PUMPKIN, CUT INTO
      WEDGES
   HONEY
   NUTMEG
   RAISINS
   SALT

Preheat oven to 350°F. On a baking sheet, bake wedges in the oven until pulp is soft. Remove skin from pulp. In a medium mixing bowl, mash with remaining ingredients according to preferences of flavors and consistency. Serve on toast or English muffins.

PREPARATION TIME: 15 MINUTES
COOKING TIME: 45 MINUTES
MAKES: 2 CUPS

PUMPKIN SEED BUTTER

½ CUP TOASTED PUMPKIN SEEDS
   SALT TO TASTE
⅓ CUP DRIED CILANTRO
3 CLOVES GARLIC, MINCED
⅓ CUP SOFT BUTTER
   PEPPER TO TASTE

Place seeds, salt, and cilantro in a blender or food processor. Add garlic, butter, and blend well. Add pepper. Serve at room temperature. Refrigerate surplus.

PREPARATION TIME: 30 MINUTES
MAKES: 1 CUP

CHAPTER 13

DESSERTS & OTHER SWEETS

Sugar plums have nothing over squashes when it comes to sweets. Cakes, candies, cookies, custards, marmalades, mousses, parfaits, pies, puddings, and tarts may all be made with products of the squash patch.

The pumpkin has been featured as a dessert primarily in pie form for as long as the history of this country has been recorded. However, there are many other ways to use this versatile cucurbit as the following recipes indicate.

Summer squash is usually overlooked when desserts are concocted, probably because it is so useful and versatile in other types of dishes. Several zucchini dessert recipes are included, therefore, as an indication that zucchini and other summer cousins should not be ignored when sweets are served.

PUMPKIN CHEESECAKE

4 8-OUNCE PACKAGES CREAM
      CHEESE, SOFTENED
1 CUP GRANULATED SUGAR
½ CUP PACKED BROWN SUGAR
5 EGGS, BEATEN
2 CUPS COOKED AND DRAINED
      PUMPKIN
1 TEASPOON GROUND CINNAMON
½ TEASPOON GROUND GINGER
¼ TEASPOON GROUND CLOVES
1 TEASPOON VANILLA EXTRACT
1 9-INCH GRAHAM CRACKER
      CRUST
   WHIPPED CREAM (OPTIONAL)

Preheat oven to 325°F. Place cream cheese in a large mixing bowl and beat in both sugars until mixture is fluffy. Add eggs gradually. Mix in remaining ingredients.

Pour batter into pie crust. Bake for 1 hour 20 minutes, or until cheesecake is firm around edges. Turn off heat and let cake remain in the *cooling* oven an additional *30 minutes.*

Cool on a wire rack. May be topped with whipped cream.

PREPARATION TIME: 10 MINUTES
BAKING TIME: 1 HOUR 20 MINUTES
MAKES: 9-INCH CHEESECAKE

PUMPKIN CUPCAKES

1 CUP COOKED AND DRAINED
      PUMPKIN
1 CUP BISCUIT MIX
¼ CUP VEGETABLE OIL
½ CUP PACKED BROWN SUGAR
2 EGGS, BEATEN
2 TEASPOONS BAKING POWDER
½ CUP MILK
½ CUP RAISINS
   BUTTER, HONEY, CREAM
      CHEESE (OPTIONAL)

Preheat oven to 350°F. In a large mixing bowl, combine all ingredients and mix thoroughly.

Fill well-greased muffin tins two-thirds full. Bake for 15-20 minutes. Place on wire racks to cool. Serve with butter, honey, or cream cheese.

PREPARATION TIME: 15 MINUTES
BAKING TIME: 15-20 MINUTES
MAKES: 24 CUPCAKES

PUMPKIN FUDGE

2 CUPS SUGAR
3 TABLESPOONS PUMPKIN PULP
¼ TEASPOON CORNSTARCH
⅓ TEASPOON PUMPKIN PIE SPICE
½ CUP MILK, EVAPORATED MILK, OR CREAM
½ TEASPOON VANILLA EXTRACT

Combine the first five ingredients in a large saucepan and cook until the mixture passes the "fudge test." This test involves dropping a small amount into cold water and if it forms a ball, the test is passed.

Then add the vanilla and beat with electric mixer until smooth. Pour onto a well-greased baking sheet or platter and cut when cool.

PREPARATION TIME: 25 MINUTES
COOKING TIME: VARIABLE
MAKES: 1 POUND

ZUCCHINI BARS

½ CUP MELTED MARGARINE
½ CUP VEGETABLE OIL
1½ CUPS PACKED BROWN SUGAR
2 EGGS
2 TABLESPOONS WATER
1 TEASPOON VANILLA EXTRACT
¼ TEASPOON GROUND NUTMEG
1½ CUPS ALL-PURPOSE FLOUR
½ CUP WHOLE-WHEAT FLOUR
⅓ TEASPOON SALT
1 TEASPOON BAKING SODA
1 CUP RAISINS
1 CUP SHREDDED COCONUT
1½ CUPS BRAN CEREAL BUDS
2½ CUPS GRATED AND DRAINED ZUCCHINI

Preheat oven to 350°F. In a large mixing bowl, mix margarine, oil, and brown sugar. Beat eggs and combine with water, vanilla, and nutmeg. Add to brown sugar mixture.

In a medium mixing bowl, sift flours, salt, and baking soda and add to brown sugar mixture. Stir in remaining ingredients.

Spread into a well-greased 12 x 8-inch baking pan. Bake for 40 minutes. Cool before cutting.

PREPARATION TIME: 15 MINUTES
BAKING TIME: 40 MINUTES
MAKES: 12 BARS

BUTTERNUT-APPLE CRISP BARS

3   CUPS PEELED AND SLICED
       BUTTERNUT SQUASH
3   CUPS PEELED AND SLICED TART
       APPLES
1   CUP PACKED BROWN SUGAR
⅛   TEASPOON GROUND CLOVES
1   TEASPOON GROUND CINNAMON
2   TEASPOONS LEMON JUICE
1¼ CUPS ALL-PURPOSE FLOUR
½   TEASPOON SALT
6   TABLESPOONS SOFTENED
       MARGARINE
⅓   CUP CHOPPED NUTS
     ICE CREAM (OPTIONAL)

Preheat oven to 350°F. In a large mixing bowl, mix squash and apple slices with ½ cup brown sugar, cloves, cinnamon, and lemon juice, tossing gently. Place in a well-greased shallow baking pan and bake for 30 minutes. Remove from oven.

In a medium mixing bowl, combine remaining brown sugar, flour, salt, and margarine until crumbly. Add nuts. Spread evenly in the baking pan. Bake for 40 minutes longer. Cut into bars. May be topped with ice cream.

PREPARATION TIME: 20 MINUTES
COOKING TIME: 1 HOUR 10 MINUTES TOTAL
MAKES: 6 BARS

RAISIN-PUMPKIN COOKIES

2½ CUPS ALL-PURPOSE FLOUR
½   TEASPOON SALT
½   TEASPOON BAKING SODA
¼   TEASPOON GROUND CINNAMON
½   TEASPOON GROUND NUTMEG
¼   TEASPOON GROUND GINGER
½   TEASPOON VANILLA EXTRACT
¾   CUP VEGETABLE OIL
1¼ CUPS PACKED BROWN SUGAR
1   EGG
1   CUP COOKED AND MASHED
       PUMPKIN
2   CUPS RAISINS

Preheat oven to 350°F. In a large mixing bowl, sift together flour, salt, baking soda, and spices. In a separate large mixing bowl, combine vanilla, oil, brown sugar, egg, and pumpkin and beat well. Add flour mixture and raisins. Mix well.

Drip spoonsful of batter on a well-greased baking sheet, allowing room for expansion. Bake for 20 minutes, or until cookies are browned.

PREPARATION TIME: 15 MINUTES
BAKING TIME: 20 MINUTES
MAKES: 48 COOKIES

CARAMELIZED PUMPKIN CUSTARD

1   CUP SUGAR
2   EGGS
1   CUP COOKED PUMPKIN
½   CUP PACKED BROWN SUGAR
½   TEASPOON GROUND CINNAMON
¼   TEASPOON GROUND GINGER
1   CUP MILK

Preheat oven to 350°F. In a small saucepan, make caramel by heating and stirring sugar over medium heat until melted. Pour into a well-greased 9 x 5-inch loaf pan.

In a medium mixing bowl, beat eggs with remaining ingredients, blending thoroughly. Pour mixture over caramelized sugar. Place custard pan in a larger pan of hot water. Bake until custard is set. Test with knife. Custard will need to bake about 1 hour. Chill.

To serve, loosen edge of custard with knife. Place a lid over custard pan and invert quickly. Individual custard cups may be used if preferred, and it may be made without caramel. Cooked winter squash may be added to any custard. Just decrease milk one-half cup for each cup of squash.

PREPARATION TIME: 20 MINUTES
BAKING TIME: 1 HOUR
SERVES: 4

PUMPKIN PARFAIT

1   3-OUNCE PACKAGE VANILLA
    PUDDING MIX
¼   CUP PACKED LIGHT BROWN
    SUGAR
½   TEASPOON GROUND CINNAMON
¼   TEASPOON GROUND GINGER
1½ CUPS MILK
1   CUP COOKED AND MASHED
    PUMPKIN
    WHIPPED CREAM (OPTIONAL)

Combine dry ingredients in a small mixing bowl.

In a large saucepan, heat milk to boiling. Add pumpkin and dry ingredients. Mix well. Spoon into serving glasses. Top with whipped cream if desired.

PREPARATION TIME: 10 MINUTES
COOKING TIME: 10 MINUTES
SERVES: 4

ZUCCHINI MARMALADE

6 CUPS TRIMMED AND SLICED
   SMALL ZUCCHINI
2 LEMONS (JUICE, PLUS 1
   TEASPOON GRATED PEEL)
1 13½-OUNCE CAN CRUSHED
   PINEAPPLE, DRAINED
1 1¾-OUNCE PACKAGE POWDERED
   FRUIT PECTIN
5 CUPS SUGAR
2 TABLESPOONS CRYSTALLIZED
   GINGER

In a large saucepan, combine zucchini, lemon juice, lemon peel, and pineapple. Bring mixture to a boil, reduce heat, and simmer uncovered about 15 minutes. Zucchini should not be allowed to become mushy.

Add pectin. Bring to a boil again. Add sugar and ginger. Bring to a rolling boil. Stirring constantly, continue boiling for 1 minute.

Remove from heat. Skim off foam. Allow mixture to cool somewhat. Ladle into hot sterilized half-pint glass jars and seal.

PREPARATION TIME: 15 MINUTES
COOKING TIME: 25 MINUTES
MAKES: 5 HALF-PINT JARS

PUMPKIN MOUSSE

2 ENVELOPES UNFLAVORED
   GELATIN
½ CUP BRANDY
½ CUP PACKED BROWN SUGAR
½ CUP GRANULATED SUGAR
1 TEASPOON GROUND CINNAMON
1 TEASPOON GROUND NUTMEG
½ TEASPOON GROUND CLOVES
½ TEASPOON SALT
2 CUPS COOKED AND MASHED
   PUMPKIN
1 CUP MILK
2 CUPS WHIPPING CREAM

Sprinkle gelatin over brandy in the top of a double boiler. Add both sugars and spices and heat until gelatin is dissolved. Add pumpkin and milk. Mix thoroughly and chill until mixture thickens.

Beat whipping cream until peaks form. Fold into pumpkin mixture. Pour into lightly greased 4-cup mold.

PREPARATION TIME: 20 MINUTES
COOKING TIME: 10 MINUTES
SERVES: 4

WINTER SQUASH PIE

1½ CUPS COOKED WINTER SQUASH
    OR PUMPKIN
1 CUP EVAPORATED MILK
3 EGGS, BEATEN
¼ CUP RUM
½ TEASPOON VANILLA EXTRACT
¾ CUP GRANULATED SUGAR
4 TABLESPOONS BROWN SUGAR
1 TEASPOON GROUND CINNAMON
½ TEASPOON GROUND GINGER
½ TEASPOON SALT
1 10-INCH PIE SHELL, BAKED

Preheat oven to 300°F. In a large mixing bowl, combine squash, milk, eggs, rum, and vanilla. Mix thoroughly.

Stir in all other ingredients. Pour batter into prepared pie shell. Bake 1 hour.

PREPARATION TIME: 25 MINUTES
BAKING TIME: 1 HOUR
SERVES: 8

BUTTERNUT CUSTARD PIE

2 EGGS, BEATEN
½ TEASPOON GROUND CINNAMON
½ TEASPOON GROUND ALLSPICE
¼ TEASPOON GROUND CLOVES
¾ CUP PACKED BROWN SUGAR
1¼ CUPS HALF-AND-HALF
¼ CUP DARK CORN SYRUP
1 TEASPOON SALT
2 CUPS COOKED AND MASHED
    BUTTERNUT SQUASH
1 9-INCH PIE SHELL, BAKED

Preheat oven to 400°F. Beat all ingredients together in a large mixing bowl.

Pour into prepared pie shell. Pour any leftover filling into custard cups. Bake at 400°F. for 10 minutes, then at 350°F. for 50 minutes until custard is set.

PREPARATION TIME: 15 MINUTES
BAKING TIME: 1 HOUR TOTAL
SERVES: 8

PUMPKIN CHIFFON PIE

1   ENVELOPE UNFLAVORED
       GELATIN
¾   CUP PACKED BROWN SUGAR
½   TEASPOON SALT
½   TEASPOON GROUND GINGER
¼   TEASPOON GROUND NUTMEG
1   TEASPOON GROUND CINNAMON
½   CUP MILK
2   CUPS COOKED AND MASHED
       PUMPKIN
2   EGG YOLKS, BEATEN
1   TEASPOON VANILLA EXTRACT
2   EGG WHITES, STIFFLY BEATEN
½   CUP WHIPPING CREAM
⅓   CUP GRANULATED SUGAR
1   9-INCH GRAHAM CRACKER
       CRUST
       ADDITIONAL WHIPPED CREAM
       (OPTIONAL)

In a large saucepan, combine gelatin, brown sugar, seasonings, milk, pumpkin, and egg yolks. Bring to a boil while stirring. Allow to cool. Add vanilla. Fold in egg whites.

In a small mixing bowl, whip cream, gradually adding sugar, until stiff. Fold into pumpkin mixture.

Pour into the crust and chill until firm. Garnish with additional whipped cream if desired.

> PREPARATION TIME: 25 MINUTES
> COOKING TIME: 10 MINUTES
> SERVES: 8

PUMPKIN ICE CREAM PIE

1½   **CUPS COOKED, MASHED, AND DRAINED PUMPKIN**
½   **CUP PACKED BROWN SUGAR**
¼   **TEASPOON SALT**
½   **TEASPOON GROUND CINNAMON**
¼   **TEASPOON GROUND NUTMEG**
¼   **TEASPOON GROUND GINGER**
1   **QUART VANILLA ICE CREAM, SOFTENED**
1   **9-INCH GRAHAM CRACKER CRUST**
¼   **CUP CHOPPED TOASTED NUTS**
  WHIPPED CREAM (OPTIONAL)

In a medium mixing bowl, combine first six ingredients. Fold into ice cream.

Spoon into pie crust. Sprinkle with nuts. May be garnished with whipped cream.

PREPARATION TIME: 15 MINUTES
SERVES: 8

STEAMED PUMPKIN PUDDING

1   **CUP COOKED AND MASHED PUMPKIN OR SQUASH**
1½   **CUPS ALL-PURPOSE FLOUR**
½   **CUP GRANULATED SUGAR**
½   **CUP PACKED BROWN SUGAR**
1   **TEASPOON BAKING SODA**
2   **TABLESPOONS ORANGE JUICE**
¾   **TEASPOON GROUND CINNAMON**
½   **TEASPOON GROUND CLOVES**
¼   **TEASPOON GROUND GINGER**
½   **TEASPOON GROUND NUTMEG**
¼   **CUP RAISINS**
⅓   **CUP MARGARINE**
1   **EGG**
¼   **CUP MILK**
  WATER

Lightly grease individual ramekins or one 6½-cup mold. In a large mixing bowl, combine all ingredients and beat thoroughly with electric mixer.

Pour mixture into ramekins until one-half full. Cover with foil and tie securely.

Place ramekins on a wire rack in a large kettle with ½-inch water. Cover and steam until pudding sets, about 15 minutes.

PREPARATION TIME: 20 MINUTES
COOKING TIME: 15 MINUTES
SERVES: 6

PUERTO RICAN PUMPKIN PUDDING

1 TABLESPOON SALT
3 EGGS
2 TABLESPOONS MARGARINE
½ TEASPOON GROUND CINNAMON
½ TEASPOON GROUND NUTMEG
⅓ CUP ALL-PURPOSE FLOUR
⅓ CUP SUGAR
⅓ CUP CREAM
2 POUNDS PUMPKIN, COOKED AND
   MASHED

Preheat oven to 400°F. In a large mixing bowl, combine all ingredients except pumpkin and mix well. Fold pumpkin into combined ingredients.

Pour mixture into a well-greased 9 x 13-inch baking dish or individual ramekins. Bake for 45 minutes.

PREPARATION TIME: 15 MINUTES
BAKING TIME: 45 MINUTES
SERVES: 12

PUMPKIN-NUT TARTS

1½ CUPS COOKED AND MASHED
    PUMPKIN
1½ CUPS MILK
1 3-OUNCE PACKAGE VANILLA
   PUDDING MIX
⅓ CUP PACKED BROWN SUGAR
½ TEASPOON GROUND CINNAMON
½ TEASPOON GROUND GINGER
8 4-INCH INDIVIDUAL TART
   SHELLS, BAKED

TOPPING:

⅓ CUP ORANGE MARMALADE
¼ CUP PACKED BROWN SUGAR
1 CUP CHOPPED NUTS

Combine all ingredients except topping ingredients in a large saucepan and bring to a boil, stirring constantly. Pour into prepared tart shells and chill.

Topping:

Combine orange marmalade and brown sugar in a small saucepan. Heat, while stirring, until brown sugar dissolves. Simmer 3 minutes. Add nuts. Spoon topping on warm tarts at serving time.

PREPARATION TIME: 20 MINUTES
COOKING TIME: 15 MINUTES
SERVES: 8

INDEX